MW00804930

HUB-E-RASUL

DIVINELY PRAISING
UPON THE
PEARL OF CREATION

*Distinguished Collection
of Arabic Salawats &
Urdu Nasheeds with Translation*

Published and Distributed by:

Sufi Meditation Center Society
3660 East Hastings
Vancouver, BC V5K 2A9 Canada
Tel: (604) 558-4455

nurmuhammad.com

First Edition: June 2018

TABLE OF CONTENTS

Salatul Mahd
صَلَاةُ الْمَهْدْ

اَللَّهُمَّ صَلِّي وَسَلِّمْ عَلَي نَبِيِّنَا مُحَمَّدْ عَلَيْهِ السَّلَامْ.
صَلَاةً تَدُوْمُ وَ تُهْدَى إِلَيه،
مَامَّرَالْلَيَالِي وَطُوْلَ دَوَامْ.

Allahumma salli wa sallim 'ala
Nabiyina Muhammad 'Alayhis Salaam.
Salatan tadumu wa tuhda ilayh,
Mammaral layali wa tula dawam.

Oh Allah (AJ), send peace and blessings upon our Prophet Muhammad, peace be upon him (pbuh). Blessings that repeat continuously and are presented to him, as long as the days and nights pass and for eternity.

The Victory Supplication

اَعُوْذُ بِاللهِ مِنَ الشَّيْطَانِ الرَّجِيْمِ

بِسْمِ اللهِ الرَّحْمَنِ الرَّحِيْم

A'uzu Billahi Min'ash Shaitanir Rajim
Bismillahir Rahmanir Raheem

I seek refuge in Allah (AJ) from Satan, the rejected one
In the Name of Allah (AJ), the Most Compassionate, the Most Merciful

إِنَّا فَتَحْنَا لَكَ فَتْحًا مُبِينًا.

Innaa fatahna laka fatham mubina. (Surat Al Fath)
Indeed, We granted you [O Muhammad (pbuh)] a clear opening. (The Victory 48:1)

لِّيَغْفِرَ لَكَ اللَّـهُ مَا تَقَدَّمَ مِن ذَنبِكَ وَمَا تَأَخَّرَ وَيُتِمَّ نِعْمَتَهُ عَلَيْكَ وَيَهْدِيَكَ صِرَاطًا مُّسْتَقِيمًا.

Liyaghfira lakaallaahu maa taqaddama min dhanbika wa maa taakhkhara, wa yutimma ni'matahu 'alayka wa yahdiyaka siraatan mustaqima. (Surat Al Fath)
May Allah (AJ) forgive us our sins of the past and those to follow; and fulfill His favors upon us and guide us to a straight path (Holy Quran, the Victory 48:2)

وَيَنصُرَكَ اللَّـهُ نَصْرًا عَزِيزًا.

Wa yansurakAllahu nasran 'aziza. (Surat Al Fath)
And [that] may Allah (AJ) support us with a mighty victory (Holy Quran, the Victory 48:3)

لَقَدْ جَاءَكُمْ رَسُولٌ مِّنْ أَنفُسِكُمْ عَزِيزٌ عَلَيْهِ مَا عَنِتُّمْ حَرِيصٌ عَلَيْكُم بِالْمُؤْمِنِينَ رَؤُوفٌ رَّحِيمٌ.

Laqad jaa akum Rasulum min anfusikum, 'azizun 'alayhi maa 'anittum harisun 'alaykum, bilmuminina Raufun Rahim. (Surat At Tawba)
There has certainly come to you a Messenger [Muhammad (saws)], among/within yourselves; you are dear to him. It grieves him to see you oppress yourself and be in difficulty. To the people of faith whom love Prophet (pbuh) more than themselves, he is most affectionate and merciful. (The Repentance 9:128)

فَإِن تَوَلَّوْا فَقُلْ حَسْبِيَ اللَّـهُ لَا إِلَهَ إِلَّا هُوَ ۖ عَلَيْهِ تَوَكَّلْتُ ۖ وَهُوَ رَبُّ الْعَرْشِ الْعَظِيمِ.

Fa in tawallaw faqul hasbi yallahu la ilaha illa Hu, 'alayhi tawakkaltu, wa Huwa Rabbul 'Arshil 'azim. (Surat At Tawba)
But if they (who keep denying the truth) turn away, [O Muhammad], say, "Allah (AJ) is sufficient for me! There is no God except Him. In Him I have placed my trust and rely on, and He is the Lord of the Mighty Throne." (The Repentance 9:129)

إِنَّ اللَّهَ وَمَلَائِكَتَهُ يُصَلُّونَ عَلَى النَّبِيِّ يَا أَيُّهَا الَّذِينَ آمَنُوا صَلُّوا عَلَيْهِ وَسَلِّمُوا تَسْلِيماً.

innAllaha wa malaaikatahu yusalluna 'alan Nabiy, yaa ayyuhal ladhina aamanu sallu 'alayhi wa sallimu taslima. (Surat AlAhzab)

Allah (AJ) and His angels send blessings on the Prophet Muhammad (pbuh): O you whom believe! Send your blessings on him, and salute him with all respect. (The Combined Forces, 33:56)

اللَّهُمَّ صَلِّ عَلَى سَيِّدِنَا مُحَمَّدٍ، وَعَلَى آلِ سَيِّدِنَا مُحَمَّدٍ وَ سَلِّمْ.

Allahumma salli 'ala Sayyidina Muhammad wa 'ala aali Sayyidina Muhammad (s)

O Allah (AJ), send peace and blessings upon our Master Prophet Muhammad (pbuh) and upon his holy family

The Opening Supplication

بِسْمِ اللهِ الرَّحْمَنِ الرَّحِيْم

Bismillahir Rahmanir Raheem

In the name of Allah, the Most Compassionate, the Most Merciful

Al Fatihatu lanaa wa lakum ya hadiron

اَلْفَاتِحَةَ لَنَا وَ لَكُمْ يَا حَاضِرُونْ

(Recite) The Fatiha (the opening chapter of Holy Quran) for us and for you, O attendees together.

**Wa li waledina wa waledikum,
wa li ahlena wa li awladina**

وَ لِوَالِدِيْنَا وَ وَالِدِيْكُمْ، وَ لِأَهَالِيْنَا وَ لِأَوْلَادِنَا.

And for our parents and your parents and for our families and for our children.

Wa li Mashayekhina wa liman hadarana wa liman ghaba 'anna

وَلِمَشَايِخِنَا وَ لِمَنْ حَضَرَنَا وَ لِمَنْ غَابَ عَنَّا.

And for our shaykhs and for whoever is attending (this gathering) with us and for whoever is absent from here.

**Wa li ahYaayena wa li amwatina,
wa lil muwazhibin 'ala hadhal majlis, wa
liman kaana sababan fi jam'enaa.**

وَلِأَحْيَائِنَا وَلَا مْوَاتِنَا وَ لِلْمَوَاظِبِيْنَ عَلَى هَذَا الْمَجْلِسِ وَ لِمَنْ كَانَ سَبَبًا فِيْ جَمْعِنَا.

And for our living ones and for our deceased ones, and for those who have prepared this gathering and for whoever was a cause for our coming.

**Bi annAllahal Karim yunawwiral qulob, wa
yaghfiradh dhunub, wa yasturul 'uyyub, wa
yahfazuna bima hafizza bihidh dhikr, wa
yansurana bima nasara bihir rusul.**

بِأَنَّ اللهَ الْكَرِيْمَ يُنَوِّرَ الْقُلُوْبَ، وَ يَغْفِرَ الذُّنُوْبَ، وَيَسْتُرُ الْعُيُوْبَ وَ يَحْفَظُنَا بِمَا حَفِظَ بِهِ الذِّكْر وَيَنْصُرَنَا بِمَا نَصَرَ بِهِ الرُّسُلَ.

That may Allah (AJ) the most Generous enlighten the hearts, and forgive the sins, and cover our shortcomings and bad characters. And that He protect us by means of whatever the remembrance protects. And He supports and gives us victory by the same means He supported and gave victory to His prophets.

**Wa annAllahal karima yaj'al majlisanaa
hadha muhaatan bil khairat, wal masarraat,
wal anwari wal barakaat, wa yaqdi lana
jami'il hajaat, bijahi khairil bariyat.**

وَ أَنَّ اللهَ الْكَرِيْمَ يَجْعَلْ مَجْلِسَنَا هَذَا مُحَاطًا بِالْخَيْرَاتِ وَالْمَسَرَّاتِ وَالْأَنْوَارِ وَالْبَرَكَاتِ. وَ يَقْضِيْ لَنَا جَمِيْعَ الْحَاجَاتِ، بِجَاهِ خَيْرِ الْبَرِيَاتِ.

Hub e Rasul | Shaykh Nurjan Mirahmadi | www.nurmuhammad.com | staffsmc@gmail.com

And that Allah (AJ) the Most Generous cause this gathering to be encompassed by goodness and happiness and lights and blessings. And that He grant us all that we are in need of, for the sake of the Best of all creation, Sayyidina Muhammad (pbuh).

Wa annAllaha yansural Muslimin.

وَأَنَّ اللهَ يَنْصُرَ الْمُسْلِمِيْنَ.

And that Allah (AJ) will support and give victory to those who submit (to Him).

Wa 'ala niyyati annAllahal Karima yansura Sultanal Awliya Mawlana Shaykh Muhammaad Nazim 'Adil, Qadas sallahu sirru, bi jahi khairil anam.

وَعَلَى نِيَّة أَنَّ اللهَ الْكَرِيْمَ يَنْصُرَ سُلْطَانَ الْأَوْلِيَاء مَوْلَانَا شَيخْ مُحَمَّدْ نَاظِمْ عَادِلَ قَدَسَّ اللهُ سِرُّ، بِجَاهِ خَيْرِ الْأَنَامِ.

And with the intention that Allah (AJ) the Most Generous support our master the Sultan of Saints, Mawlana Shaykh Muhammad Nazim 'Adil, May Allah (AJ) sanctify his secret, for the sake of the Best of all creation.

Wa 'ala kulli niyyatin saalihatin ma'a husnil khatimati 'indal mawti b'adal umril madid fi Ta'atillah wa ila hadratin Nabiyyi.
Bi siri Suratul Fatiha.

وَعَلَى كُلّ نِيَّة صَالِحَة مَعْ حُسْنِ الْخَاتِمَة عِنْدَالْمَوْتِ بَعْدَ الْعُمْرِ الْمَدِيدِ فِيْ طَاعَة اللهِ وَ إِلَي حَضْرَةِ النَّبِيّ. بِسِرِّ سُوْرَةُالْفَاتِحَةَ !

And on every pure intention with most perfect of endings at the time of passing from this life, after a long life in service and obedience to Allah (AJ) and to the ever-present Prophet (Sayyidina Muhammad (pbuh)). By the secrets of the chapter of Al Fatiha. [Recite the first chapter of Holy Quran, Al Fatiha (The Opener)].

بِسْمِ اللهِ الرَّحْمَنِ الرَّحِيْم

اَنْتَ سُلْطَانُنَا يَا رَبَّنَا، اِغْفِرْلَنَا وَارْحَمْنَا وَ ثُبْ عَلَيْنَا،
وَزِدْ حَبِيْبِكَ سَيِّدِ الْأَوَّلِيْنْ وَالْأَخِرِينْ
سَيِّدِنَا مُحَمَدْ (صَلَي اللهُ عَلَيْهِ وَ سَلَّمْ)!
زِدْ هُوْ يَا رَبِّي عِزّاً وَشَرَفاً و نُوراً وَ سُرُوراً و سُلْطَاناً وَ رِضْوَاناً.
رَغْماً عَلَي أَنْفِ الشَّيْطَانْ وَمَنْ تَبِعَهُ.

Bismillahir Rahmanir Raheem

Anta Sultanuna ya Rabbana,
Ighfir lana, warhamna, wa tub 'alayna,
wa zid habibika, Sayyidul Awwaleen wal Akhireen,
Sayyidina Muhammad (SallAllahu 'Alayhi Wa sallam).
ZidHu Ya Rabbi 'Izzan wa sharafan, wa Nooran wa surooran,
wa Sultanan wa ridwaana.
Raghman 'ala anfish Shaytan wa man tabi 'ahu.

In the name of Allah (AJ), the Most Compassionate, the Most Merciful

O our Lord, you are our King!
Forgive us, and have mercy on us, and grant us repentance.
And raise Your Beloved, our leader and master, the first of Allah's (AJ) creation and the seal of Allah's (AJ) messengers, our Master Prophet Muhammad (pbuh). O my Lord, increase his nobility, his honour, his light and happiness, and expand his kingdom on earth and heavens, despite the devil and his followers.

Ibadallah Rijal Allah

عِبَادَ الله رِجَالَ الله

عِبَادَ الله رِجَالَ الله
وَكُونُوا عَوْنَنَا فِي الله

أَغِيثُونَا بِأَهْلِ الله
عَسَى نَحْظَى بِفَضْلِ الله

Ibadallah Rijal Allah
Wa kunu 'aunana fillah

Agheethuna bi ahlillah
'Asa nahzha bi fadlilla

O servants of Allah (AJ), O men of Allah (AJ), Bring us relief, by the People of Allah (AJ)
And help us for the sake of Allah (AJ), so we may receive the favours of Allah (AJ)

وَيَاأَقْطَاب وَيَاأَنْجَاب
وَأَنْتُمْ يَاأُولِى الْأَلْبَاب

وَيَا سَادَاتْ وَيَاأَحْبَاب
تَعَالُوا وَانْصُرُوالله

Wa ya AqTab, wa ya Anjab
Wa antum ya Ulil albab

Wa ya Sadat, wa ya Ahbab
Ta'alau wan suru lillah

O Pillars of religion, O generous men, O Masters, O lovers of Prophet Muhammad (saws),
You are the Heavenly gate keepers, Come to our rescue and make us victorious

CHORUS

سَأَلْنَاكُمْ سَأَلْنَاكُمْ
وَفِيْ أَمْرٍ قَصَدنَاكُمْ

وَلِلزُلفَى رَجَوْنَاكُمْ
فَشُدُّو أَمْرَكُمْ لله

Sa alnakum, sa alnakum
Wa fee amrin qasad nakum

Wa lizzulfa rajau nakum
Fa shuddu amrakum lillah

We ask from you, we entreat you, We set our hearts on your companionship,
And for important matters we call up on you; So, we come with humility to answer
the command of Allah (AJ)

CHORUS

فَيَا رَبِّى بِسَادَاتِيْ
عَسَى تَأْتِى بِشَارَتِيْ

تَحَقَّقْ لِى إِشَارَتِيْ
وَيَصْفُو أَمْرُنَا لله

Faya rabbi, bi sadatee
'Asa ta'tee bi sharatee

Tahaqqaq li isharatee
Wa yasfu amruna lillah

O Lord, by these Masters, Your signs have been confirmed, We are hoping to witness glad tidings. And that they guide us, cleanse us, and keep us firm on our path

CHORUS

وَرَفْعِ الْبَيْنِ مِنْ بَيْنِي
بِنُورِ الْوَجْهِ يَا الله

بِكَشْفِ الْحُجْبِ عَنْ عَيْنِيْ
وَ صَرْفِ الْقَلْبِ وَالْعَيْنِيْ

Bi kashfil hujbi 'an 'ainee
Wa sarfil qalbi wal 'ainee

Wa raf'il baini min bainee
BiNuril wajhi ya Allah

Lift the veils that are covering my sight, And remove anything that is blocking me from You, grant me the abode of your presence, which is the desire of my heart and eyes, By the light of the holy face of (Prophet (pbuh)), O Allah (AJ)

CHORUS

عَلَى مَنْ بِالْهُدَا جَانَا
شَفِيعِ الْخَلْقِ عِنْدَ الله

صَلَاةُ الله مَوْلَانَا
وَمَنْ بِالْحَقِّ أَوْلَانَا

Salatullahi Mawlana
Wa man bil haqqi awlana

'Ala man bil Huda jana
Shafi'il khalqi 'indallah

May the blessings of our Lord Allah (AJ), Be upon Prophet Muhammad (pbuh), who guided us to the right path; He who entrusted us with His religion of Truth, He is the Intercessor for all human beings, in front of Allah (AJ)

CHORUS

اَللّٰهُمَّ صَلِّ وَ سَلِّمْ وَ بَارِكْ عَلَيْهِ وَ عَلَى آلِهْ
Allahuma salli wa sallim wa barik 'alayhi wa 'ala alih
O Allah (AJ) send peace and blessings upon Prophet Muhammad (pbuh) and his family.

Madad (Seeking Support)

مَدَدْ

(Seeking Support from the MaShaykh (Masters))

مَدَدْ، مَدَدْ، مَدَدْ

يا سَيِّدِيْ مَدَدْ   مَدَدْ يَا رَسُوْلَ الله

Madad, Madad, Madad
Ya Sayyidi Madad   Madad, Ya Rasul Allah

1. Madad Ya Abubakr Siddiq   ١ . مَدَدْ يَا أَبُوْبَكْرصِدِّيْقُ
2. Madad Ya Umar Farooq   ٢ . مَدَدْ يَاعُمَرْفَارُوْق
3. Madad Ya Uthman Ghani   ٣ . مَدَدْ يَاعُثْمَانْ غَنِيْ
4. Madad Ya Imam Ali   ٤ . مَدَدْ يَا إِمَامْ عَلِيْ

CHORUS

- Madad Ya Fatima Zahra   . مَدَدْ يَا فَاطِمَة زَهْرَا
- Madad Ya Imam Hassan   . مَدَدْ يَا إِمَامْ حَسَّنْ
- Madad Ya Imam Hussain   . مَدَدْ يَا إِمَامْ حُسَّيْنْ
- Madad Ya Salman Farsi   . مَدَدْ يَا سَلْمَانْ فَارْسِيْ

CHORUS

Madad Ya Qaasimoo   . مَدَدْ يَا قَاسِمُ

Madad Ya Saadiqoo   . مَدَدْ يَاصَادِقُ

Madad Ya Bistami   . مَدَدْ يَا بِسْطَامِيْ

Madad Ya Kharqani   . مَدَدْ يَا خَرْقَانِيْ

CHORUS

Madad Ya Farmadi   . مَدَدْ يَا فَارْمَادِئ

Madad Ya Hamadani   . مَدَدْ يَا هَمَدَانِيْ

Madad Ya Khidroo   . مَدَدْ يَا خِضْرُوْ

Madad Ya Ghujdawani   . مَدَدْ يَا غُجْدَوَانِيْ

Madad Ya 'Arifoon   . مَدَدْ يَا عَارِفُوْنْ

Madad Ya Faghnawi   . مَدَدْ يَا فَغْنَوِئ

CHORUS

Madad Ya Ramitanee   . مَدَدْ يَا رَمِيْتَانِيْ

Madad Ya Samasi   . مَدَدْ يَا سَمَاسِيْ

Madad Ya Amir Kulal   . مَدَدْ يَا آمِيْر كُلَالْ

Madad Ya Shah Naqshband	مَدَدْ يَا شَاه النَّقشبَند .
Madad Ya 'Attaru	مَدَدْ يَا عَطَارُوْ .
Madad Ya Charkhi	مَدَدْ يَا چَرْخِىْ .

CHORUS

Madad Ya Ahrari	مَدَدْ يَا اَحْرَارِيْ .
Madad Ya Zahidi	مَدَدْ يَا ذَاهِدِئْ .
Madad Ya Darwishoo	مَدَدْ يَا دَرْوِيْشُ .
Madad Ya Amkanaki	مَدَدْ يَا اَمْكَنَكِىْ .
Madad Ya Baqi billah	مَدَدْ يَا بَاقِىْ بِالله .
Madad Ya Sirhindi	مَدَدْ يَا سِرْهِنْدِئْ .

CHORUS

Madad Ya M'asumi	مَدَدْ يَا مَعْصُومِيْ .
Madad Ya Saifuddin	مَدَدْ يَا سَيْفُالدّينْ .
Madad Ya Badwani	مَدَدْ يَا بَدْوَانِىْ .
Madad Ya Shamsuddin	مَدَدْ يَا شَمْسُالدّينْ .
Madad Ya Dahlawi	مَدَدْ يَادَهْلَوِئْ .
Madad Ya Baghdadi	مَدَدْ يَا بَغْدَادِئْ .

CHORUS

Madad Ya Isma'il	مَدَدْ يَا إِسْمَاعِيْلْ .
Madad Ya Khas Muhammad	مَدَدْ يَا خَاصْ مُحَمَّدْ .
Madad Ya Yaraghi	مَدَدْ يَا يَرَأغِىْ .
Madad Ya Ghumuqi	مَدَدْ يَا غُمُوقِى .

CHORUS

Madad Ya Sughuri	مَدَدْ يَا سُغُوْرِئْ .
Madad Ya Madani	مَدَدْ يَا مَدَنِىْ .
Madad Ya Sharafuddin	مَدَدْ يَا شَرَفُالدّينْ .
Madad Ya 'Abdullah	مَدَدْ يَا عَبْدُالله .

CHORUS

Madad Ya Shaykh Nazim	مَدَدْ يَا شَيخ نَاظِمْ
Madad Ya Shaykh Hisham	مَدَدْ يَا شِيخْ هِشَامْ
Madad Ya Shaykh 'Adnan	مَدَدْ يَا شِيخْ عَدْنَانْ
Madad Ya Shaykh Muhammad Adil	مَدَدْ يَا شِيخْ مُحَمَّدْ عَادِلْ

CHORUS

Madad Ya Sahibul Waqt   15   مَدَدْ يَا صَاحِبُ الْوَقْتِ

1. Madad Ya Fardani   ١. مَدَدْ يَا فَرْدَانِیْ
2. Madad Ya Siddiqoon   ٢. مَدَدْ يَاصِدِّيْقُوْن
3. Madad Ya Yamani   ٣. مَدَدْ يَا يَمَنِیْ
4. Madad Ya Imamul 'Arifeen   ٤. مَدَدْ يَا إِمَامُ الْعَارِفِیْن
5. Madad Ya Sakhawi   ٥. مَدَدْ يَا سَخَاوِیْ
6. Madad Ya M'aruf bi Mulhan   ٦. مَدَدْ يَا مَعْرُوْفُ بِمُلْحَانْ
7. Madad Ya Ghawthil Anam   ٧. مَدَدْ يَا غَوْثِ الْأَ نَامْ

(إِمَامُ الْمِهْدِي خَلِيْفَةُ اللهِ) x ٢

Imam Mahdi Khalifa tullahi x2

Part A

The Opening Qasida
قَصِيْدَةُ الْإِفْتِتَاحْ

يَا رَبِّي صَلِّ عَلَى مُحَمَّدْ
(يَا رَبِّي صَلِّ عَلَيْهِ وَ سَلِمْ) ٢x

**(Ya Rabbi salli 'ala Muhammad
Ya Rabbi salli 'alayhi wa sallim) x2**

O my Lord, bestow blessings upon our Master Prophet Muhammad (pbuh),
O my Lord, bestow peace and blessings upon him (pbuh)

يَا رَبِّي بَلِّغْهُ الْوَسِيْلَة
يَا رَبِّي وَارْضَ عَنِ الصَّحَابَة

**Ya Rabbi khussaHu bil fadilah
Ya Rabbi warda 'anis Sulalah**

يَا رَبِّي خُصَّ هُوْ بِالْفَضِيْلَة
يَا رَبِّي وَارْضَ عَنِ السُّلَا لَة

**Ya Rabbi ballighul wasilah
Ya Rabbi warda 'anis Sahabah**

O my Lord, grant us his intercession and make him a means for us to approach You, O my Lord, raise his honour and station even higher, You are with his holy companions, and his descendents

CHORUS

يَا رَبِّي وَارْضَ عَنِ الْمَشَايِخْ
يَا رَبِّي وَارْحَمْنَا جَمِيْعًا

**Ya Rabbi farham walidina
Ya Rabbi warham kulla Muslim**

يَا رَبِّي فَارْحَمْ وَالِدِيْنَا
يَا رَبِّي وَارْحَمْ كُلَّ مُسْلِمْ

**Ya Rabbi warda anil mashayikh
Ya Rabbi warhamna jami'an**

O my Lord, be pleased with all the masters and spiritual guides, O my Lord, have mercy on our parents, on those who submit and have mercy on all of us

CHORUS

يَا رَبِّي وَاغْفِرْ لِكُلِّ مُذْنِبْ
يَا رَبِّي لَا تَقْطَعْ رَجَانَا

**Ya Rabbi ya sami' du'ana
Ya Rabbi ballighna nazuruh**

يَا رَبِّي يَا سَامِعْ يَا سَامِعْ دُعَانَا
يَا رَبِّي بَلِغْنَا نَزُوْرُهْ

**Ya Rabbi waghfir li kulli mudhnib
Ya Rabbi la taqt'a rajana**

O my Lord, forgive all sinners, O my Lord, O Hearer of our plea/prayer! Do not cut us from our salvation and grant us a visit to Prophet Muhammad's (pbuh) resting place in Madinatul Munawara

CHORUS

Hub e Rasul | Shaykh Nurjan Mirahmadi | www.nurmuhammad.com | staffsmc@gmail.com

يَا رَبِّي تَغْشَانَا بِنُورِهْ
يَا رَبِّي وَاسْكِنَّا جِنَانَكْ

يَا رَبِّي حِفْظَاتَكْ وَ اَمَانَكْ
يَا رَبِّي اَجِرْنَا مِنْ عَذَابِكْ

Ya Rabbi taghshana bi nurih
Ya Rabbi waskina jinanak

Ya Rabbi hifzanak wa amanak
Ya Rabbi ajirna min 'adhabik

O my Lord, cover us with Prophet Muhammad's (pbuh) heavenly light, O my Lord, safeguard us and protect us from Your punishment, O my Lord, make Your paradise our eternal home

CHORUS

يَا رَبِّي حُطْنَا بِالسَّعَادَه
يَا رَبِّي وَاكْفِ كُلَّ مُؤْذِي

يَا رَبِّي وَارْزُقْنَا الشَّهَادَه
يَا رَبِّي وَاصْلِحْ كُلَّ مُصْلِحْ

Ya Rabbi warzuqnash shahadah
Ya Rabbi waslih kulla muslih

Ya Rabbi hutna bissa'adah
Ya Rabbi wakfi kulla mudhi

O my Lord, bless us with the station of witnessing and make us from your servants whose hearts are open. O my Lord, surround us with happiness, save us from all those whom want to harm us. O my Lord, raise our Shaykhs' and guides' stations higher and higher and give them more light and support so they raise us and guide us on our path

CHORUS

اَللَّهُمَّ صَلِّ وَ سَلِّمْ وَ بَارِكْ عَلَيْهِ وَ عَلَى اَلِهْ

Allahuma salli wa sallim wa barik 'alayhi wa 'ala alih
O Allah (AJ) send peace and blessings upon Prophet Muhammad (pbuh) and his family.

Ya Rasulullah Salamun 'Alayk

يَا رَسُولُ اللهِ سَلَامٌ عَلَيك

يَا رَسُولُ اللهِ سَلَامٌ عَلَيك
عَطْفَةً يَاجِيْرَةَ الْعَلَمِ

يَا رَفِيْعَ الشَّأَنِ وَالدَّرَج
يَا أَهَيْلَ الْجُوْدِ وَالْكَرَمِ

Ya Rasulullah, Salamun 'Alayk
'Atfatan ya jiratal 'alami

Ya Rafi 'ash shani wad daraji
Ya uhaylal judi wal karami

O Messenger of Allah (AJ), peace be upon you! O Possessor of the highest rank and station, Have sympathy for us, O distinguished neighbour, O the one who is giving & generous

نَحْنُ مِنْ قَوْمٍ بِهِ سَكَنُوْا
وَبِآيَاتِ الْقُرَآنِ عُنُوْا

وَبِهِ مِنْ خَوْفِهِمْ أَمِنُوْا
فَاتَّئِدْ فِيْنَا أَخَا الْوَهَنِ

Nahnu min qawmin bihi sakanu
Wa bi aayatil Qurani 'unu

Wa bihi min khawfihim aminu
Fattayid fina akhal wahani

We are from amongst the people, who through him reached tranquility, And through him we were saved from fear, And we have busied ourselves and became companions of holy Quran

CHORUS

نَعْرِفُ الْبَطَحَا وَتَعْرِفَنَا
وَلَنَا الْمَعْلَى وَخِيْفُ مِنَى

وَالصَّفَا وَالْبَيْتُ يَأْلَفَنَا
فَاعْلَمَّنْ هَذَا وَكُنْ رَكِن

Na'riful batha wa ta'rifuna
Wa lanal ma'la wa khifu Mena

Was-safa wal-baytu ya'lafuna
F'alaman hadha wa kun rakini

We know the desert and it knows us, And Safa and the Ka'bah sharif are familiar with us, Al Ma'la and Khifu Mena are for us, Know that and be heedful and respectful

CHORUS

Hub e Rasul | Shaykh Nurjan Mirahmadi | www.nurmuhammad.com | staffsmc@gmail.com

وَعَلِيُّ الْمُرْتَضَى حَسَبُ
نَسَبًا مَافِيهِ مِنْ دَخَنِ

وَلَنَا خَيْرُ الْأَنَامِ أَبُ
وَإِلَى السِّبْطَيْنِ نَنْتَسِبُ

Wa 'Ali ul Murtada hasabu
Nasaban ma fihi min dakhini

Wa lana khayrul anami abu
Wa ilas sibtayni nantasibu

The best of creation is our father Prophet Muhammad (pbuh), And Imam Ali (as)) the Blessed one, is our family, And we are related to the two lions (Imam Hassan and Imam Hussain (as)), There is no doubt about our lineage

CHORUS

مِنْهُ سَادَاتٌ بِذَا عُرِفُوا
مِنْ قَدِيمِ الدَّهْرِ وَالزَّمَنِ

كَمْ إِمَامٍ بَعْدَهُ خَلَفُوا
وَبِهَذَا الْوَصْفِ قَدْ وُصِفُوا

Minhu sadatun bidha 'urifu
Min qadimi dahri waz-zamani

Kam Imamin ba'dahu khalafu
Wa bi hadhal wasfi qad wusifu

How many imams (and leaders) have come from their progeny, They are the leaders of this nation as described, Since ancient time and previous eras

CHORUS

وَابْنِهِ الْبَاقِرِ خَيْرُ وَلِيْ
وَعَلِيِ ذِى الْعُلَا الْيَقِيْنِ

مِثْلُ زَيْنِ الْعَابِدِينَ عَلِيْ
وَالْإِمَامِ الصَّادِقِ الْحَفِلِ

Wabni hil Baqiri khayrul wali
Wa 'Aliyin dhil 'ulal yaqini

Mithlu Zaynil 'Aabidina 'Ali
Wal Imamis Sadiqil hafili

Like Imam Zaynul 'Aabidin 'Ali (as), And his son Imam Muhammad Baqir (as) who is the best of saints, And the honoured leader of the nation of Imam Sadiq (as), And Imam Ali Rida (as) of high station of certainty

CHORUS

وَبِفَضْلِ اللهِ قَدْ سُعِدُوا
وَمَعَ الْقُرَآنِ فِي الْقَرَنِ

فَهُمُ الْقَوْمُ الَّذِينَ هُدُوا
وَلِغَيْرِ اللهِ مَا قَصَدُوا

Wa bi fadlil lahi qad su'idu
Wa m'al Qurani fil qarani

Fahumul qawmul ladhina hudu
Wa li ghayril lahi ma qasadu

They are the people who were most rightly guided, And they were blessed with Allah's (AJ) favours, They were only seeking Allah's (AJ) satisfaction. They were companions of the holy Quran

CHORUS

أَهْلُ بَيْتِ الْمُصْطَفَى الطّهُرِ
شُبِّهُوا بِالْأَنْجُمِ الزُّهُرِ

هُمْ اَمَانُ الْأَرْضِ فَإِذْكِرِ
مِثْلَمَا قَدْ جَاءَ فِي السُّنَنِ

Ahlu baytil Mustafa tuhori
Shubihu bil anjumiz zuhuri

Hum amanul ardi f'azzakiri
Mithlama qad ja'a fi's sunani

The pure family of the Chosen One (Prophet Muhammad (pbuh)), They are the guarantee for this earth's purity so be heedful and respect them. They were described as the shining stars, As it's been related in the Prophetic traditions

CHORUS

خِفْتَ مِنْ طُوْفَانِ كُلِّ اَذَى
وَإِعْتَصِمْ بِاللهِ وَاسْتَعِنِ

وَسَفِيْنٌ لِلنّجَاةِ إِذَا
فَانْجُ فِيهَا لَا تَكُوْنَ كَذَا

Wa safi nun lin najati idha
Fanju-fiha la takunu kadha

Khifta min tufani kulli adha
W'atasim billahi wasta'ini

They are the ship of salvation, so when you are drowning in the storms of difficulties and hardship, do not be heedless. Hold onto their rope and ask for Allah's (AJ) support

CHORUS

وَاهْدِنَا الْحُسْنَى بِحُرْمَتِهِمْ
وَمَعَافَاةٍ مِنَ الْفِتَنِ

رَبِّي فَانْفَعْنَا بِبَرَكَتِهِمْ
وَأَمِتْنَا فِي طَرِيْقَتِهِمْ

Rabbi fanf'ana bi barkatihim
Wa amitna fi Tariqatihim

Wahdinal husna bi hurmatihim
Wa ma'aafatin minal fitani

My Lord benefit us through their blessings, And guide us to goodness for their respect, And let us die on their path, And to be safe from confusion

اَللّهُمَّ صَلِّ وَ سَلِّمْ وَ بَارِكْ عَلَيْهِ وَ عَلَى اَلِهْ
Allahuma salli wa sallim wa barik 'alayhi wa 'ala alih
O Allah (AJ) send peace and blessings upon Prophet Muhammad (pbuh) and his family.

Sayyidi, Ya Sayyidi

سَيِّدِيْ يَا سَيِّدِيْ

مُحَمَّدْ يَا حَبَيِّبِيْ (x ٢

(رسَيِّدِيْ يَا سَيِّدِيْ

(Sayyidi, Ya Sayyidi   Muhammad, Ya Habayibi) x2

O my Master, O my Beloved Prophet Muhammad (pbuh)

شَرَفِيْ وَعِزِّيْ وُ نِبْرَاسِيْ (x ٢
وَالله، فِيْهِ تِبَاهِيْنَا

(حُبَك، بِقَلْبِيْ رَاسِيْ
(رَافِعْ نَعْلَكْ، عَلَى رَاسِيْ) x ٢

(Hubak be qalbi rasi   Sharfi wa 'izzi o nabrasi) x2
(Rafi na'lak, 'ala rasi) x2   Wallah, fihi tibahinaa

Your love has filled and anchored my heart. You are my honour, my light. I want my head to be at your holy feet. I put your sandal and turban on my head with a lot of pride, I swear it is my crown and honour.

CHORUS

مِنْ آثَارِه وُأَحْبَابَه (x ٢
تَمَسُوا بَرَكَة، مِنْ نَبِيِّنَا

(طَالِبْ بَرَكَة جَنَابَك
(بِشْهَدْ لِيْ، فِعِلْ أَصْحَابَة) x ٢

(Talib, barkat janaba   Min atharaw, ahbaba) x2
(Ishhad li, fe'yil Ashaba) x2   Tamaso barkat, Nabyeena

I am a seeker of blessing from your eminence. I wish to follow your footsteps and the footsteps of your companions, lovers, and those who are at your threshold. I want to follow at the footsteps of the exemplars of faith, as they showed their love by action and made many sacrifices for your love, O Prophet Muhammad (pbuh)

CHORUS

فُقَهَاء وُ،سَادَة وُ بَرَرَةٌ (x ٢
هُمْ خَيْرُالْعَارِفِينَ

(وُبْحُجْرَكْ، يَا أَبَا الزَّهْرَاء
(حَنَّكْهُمْ، طَهَ بِتَّمْرَة) x ٢

(Wub hujrak, ya abaz Zahra   Fuqaha o sadaw barrah) x2
(Hannak hum, Ta habbit tamra) x2   Hum khiril 'Arifeena

O Father of Fatima Zahra (as), in your holy heart is the house of Allah (AJ). All the souls of the true guides, jurists, scholars, and pious servants are gathered in your heart. O Taha, the Purified Guide, from the realities that flow to you from the Divine presence, you fill their hearts. They are gnostics and the lovers of the Divine presence.

يُشْرَبْ، طَهَ بِالْقِرْبَة (

x۲ (تِقْطَعْ مِنْ مَوْضِعْ شُرْبَهْ)

وُصْحَابِيَّة، مِنْ حُبِّهْ) x۲

تِجْعَلْهَا، بَرَكَة وُ زِينْةَ

(Yushrab, Taha bil qerba

(Teqta min mawdeh shurbah) x2

Wushabi ya, min Hubba) x2

Tij'alha barkaw zeenaa

Taha, the Purified Guide (pbuh), drank from the Divine presence and his thirst was quenched. And his holy companions drank the oceans of realities from his holy hands. They received the highest rank, honour, and blessings through their love for the Prophet (pbuh)

CHORUS

مَا يُطْفِي الْقَلْبِ إِشْوَاقَهْ) (

x۲ (مِثِلْ أَصْحَابَهْ وُ عِشَاقَهْ)

لَأَقَبِلْ قَدَمَهْ أَوْ سَاقَهْx۲

بِالْمَحْشَرْ يِشْفَعْ لِي

(Ma yutfil, qalb ishwaqah

(Mithl, Ashaba aw Ishaqa) x2

La qabel, qadamaw saqah) x2

Bil masher Ishfa'lee

Nothing will comfort my heart, except to keep my head at your holy feet and to be on your path and to follow your way. Just the way your holy companions, the saints, and your lovers followed your way and magnificent character. Only your love will save me and intercede for me on the day of gathering and judgment day.

CHORUS

اَللّهُمَّ صَلِ وَ سَلِّمْ وَ بَارِكْ عَلَيْهِ وَ عَلَي اَلِهْ

Allahuma salli wa sallim wa barik 'alayhi wa 'ala alih

O Allah (AJ) send peace and blessings upon Prophet Muhammad (pbuh) and his family.

Ya Hannan Ya Mannan

يَا حَنَانْ يَا مَنَانْ

يَا حَنَانْ يَا مَنَانْ
بَحْرَ جُودِكَ مَلْيَانْ

يَا قَدِيمُ الْإِحْسَانْ
(جُدْ لَنَا بِالْغُفْرَانْ) x۲

Ya Qadi mul Ihsaan
(Judlana bil ghufran) x2

Ya Hannan, Ya Mannan
Bahra judik mal-yan

O Most Compassionate, O Giver, O pre-eternal Excellence,
Grant us forgiveness, felicity and contentment

جُدْ لِهَذَا الْإِنْسَانْ
مِنْ ذُنُوبِهِ وَحَلَانْ

عَبْدُ سُوءٍ خَزْيَانْ
(خَائِفْ إِنَّكَ غَضْبَانْ) x۲

Abdu suin khazyan
(Khayif innak ghadban) x2

Jud li hazal insaan
Min zunubihi wa halaan

Grant me, who is a disgraced evil doer servant, who is covered with sin,
I am ashamed of my sins and fear that You might be angry with me

CHORUS

رَبَّنَا نَسْتَعْفِيك
وَلَنَا ظَنٌّ فِيك

رَبَّنَا نَسْتَرْضِيك
(يَا رَجَاء أَهْلَ الْإِيمَان) x۲

Rabbanna nastar dheek
(Ya raja, ahlal iman) x2

Rabbanna nasta'feek
Wa lana zannun feek

O our Lord, we are asking for Your pardon, We are seeking Your satisfaction and beg
Your forgiveness, O hope of the believers

CHORUS

لَا تُخَيِّبْ رَاجِيْ
لَمْ يَزَلْ فِي الدَّاجِيْ

تَحْتَ بَابِكَ لَاجِئْ
(قَائِلاً يَا حَنَّانْ) x۲

Tahta babik laaji
(Qailan ya hannan) x2

La tokhayyib raji
Lam yazal fiddaji

Don't deny me Your mercy, I am helpless and seek refuge at Your door,
I am still lost in the darkness and confusion, I'm calling upon You, O the Most
Compassionate

CHORUS

بِالنَّبِيِّ الْأُمِّيْ
وَالْبَتُوْلِ الْخَتْمِيْ

وَخَدِيْجَةَ أُمِّيْ
(سَيِّدَاتِ النِّسْوَانْ) ٢x

Bin Nabi il ummi
Wal batulil khatmi

Wa Khadija ummi
(Sayeed-da-tin niswaan) x2

By Prophet Muhammad's (pbuh) mother [Amina (as)], And our Mother Khadija (as) [his first wife], And his beloved daughter, Fatima (as), the purified and perfected light like no other to come. They are the leaders of all women

CHORUS

بِالنَّبِيِّنْ الْأَجَمْ
وَبِنُوْحِ الْأَقْدَمْ

مِنْ أَبِيْنَا آدَمْ
(وَخَلِيْلِ الرَّحْمَنْ) ٢x

Bin Nabi yin ajam
Wa bi Nohil aqdaam

Min abina Adam
(Wa Khali lir Rahmaan) x2

By all the Prophets, from our father Adam (as), And by the courageous Prophet Noah (as), And the intimate friend of the Most Beneficent (Prophet Ibrahim (as))

CHORUS

بِأَهْلِ تُرْبَةِ بَشَارْ
وَ بِآلٍ وَ بِالْأَبْرَارْ

وَالْفَقِيْهِ الْمِشْهَارْ
(مَنْ بِهِمْ حَالِ زَانْ) ٢x

Be Ahli Tur-bashar
Wabi a'li wa bil' abarar

Wal faqihil mishhar
(Man bihim hali zan) x2

By the people of the Bashar's graveyard (place in Tarim, Yemen), and its renowned jurist. And by his family and the purified ones, with whom my life and condition got better

CHORUS

اَللّهُمَّ صَلِّ وَ سَلِّمْ وَ بَارِكْ عَلَيْهِ وَ عَلَي آلِهْ
Allahuma salli wa sallim wa barik 'alayhi wa 'ala alih
O Allah (AJ) send peace and blessings upon Prophet Muhammad (pbuh) and his family.

Salatullahi Ma Laahat Kawakeb
صَلَاةُ اللهِ مَا لَاحَتْ كَوَاكِبْ

عَلَى احْمَدْ خَيْرِ مَنْ رَكِبَ النَّجَآئِبْ   صَلَاةُ اللهِ مَالَاحَتْ كَوَاكِبْ

Salatullahi ma laahat Kawakeb
'Ala Ahmad khari man rakeban najaayeb

Allah (AJ) sends blessings as many as the stars appear in the sky,
Upon Prophet Ahmad (pbuh), the best guide in this excellent journey

فَهَزَّ السُّكُرُ اَعْطَافَ الرَّكَائِبْ   حَدَى حَادِى السُّرَى بِإِسْمِ الْحَبَآئِبْ

Hada haadis sura bismil habaayeb
Fahazzas sukru a'Taffar rakaayeb

Swaying in hearing the person who sang the praising of the beloved Prophet
Muhammad (pbuh), It touched the hearts of the travelers on the journey to Madina
Sharif and they felt sweet joy and ecstasy

CHORUS

وَسَألَتْ مِنْ مَدَامِعِهَا سَحَآئِبْ   اَلَمْ تَرَهَا وَقَدْ مَدَّتْ خُطَاهَا

Alam tarhaa wa qad maddat khuTahaa
Wa saalat min madam'yi ha sahaayeb

Did you not see how the camel in excitement took wider steps, And tears
fell down from its eyes in happiness when he got closer to Madina.

CHORUS

نَبِيٌّ نُوْرُهُوْ يَجْلُو الْغَيَاهِبْ   وَتِلْكَ الْقُبَّةَ الْخَضْرَاء وَفِيْهَا

Wa tilkal qubbatul khadra wa fihaa
Nabiyun nooruhu yajlul ghayaaheb

And that is the Green Dome, in it rests a Prophet whose light brightens and
illuminates the darkness of the world

CHORUS

فَمَا دُوْنَ الْحَبِيْبِ الْيَوْمَ حَاجِبْ   فَقُلْ لِلنَّفْسِ دُوْنَكِ وَالتَّمَلِّيْ

Faqul lin nafsi donaka wat tamalli
Famaa donal Habibil yawma haajeb

Say to yourselves, don't waste time and don't delay, Because in front of us is the Beloved of Allah (AJ). Today there is no veiling or barrier between us.

CHORUS

لَهُ أَعْلَى الْمَنَاصِبِ وَالْمَرَاتِبْ   نَبِيُّ اللهِ خَيْرُ الْخَلْقِ جَمِيْعًا

Nabiyullaahi khayrul Khalqi jami'an
Lahu a'lal manaasibi wal marateb

This is the Prophet of Allah (AJ), the best of all creation, Who has the highest rank and most honourable position in divinely presence

CHORUS

لِأَحْمَدَ مَوْلِدًا قَدْ كَانَ وَاجِبْ   وَلَوْ أَنَّا عَمِلْنَا كُلّ يَــوْمٍ

Wa lao annaa 'amilnaa kulla yawmin
Li Ahmada mawlidan qad kaana waajeb

And if every day we do this Mawlid celebration of the birth of Prophet Muhammad (pbuh). It is our obligation and duty to do so

CHORUS

صَلَاةٌ مَا بَدَا نُوْرُ الْكَوَاكِبْ   عَلَيْهِ مِنَ الْمُهَيْمِنِ كُلّ وَقْتٍ

'Alayhi minal Muhaimini kulla waqtin
Salaatun maa badaa noorul kawaakeb

Allah (AJ), the All Powerful, sends peace and blessings upon him at all times, As much as the shining lights of the stars

CHORUS

تَعُمُّ الْآلَ وَالْأَصْحَابَ طُرًّا   جَمِيعَهُمْ وَعِتْرَتَهُ الْأَطَايِبْ

Ta'ummul aala wal as-haaba Turran
Jami'ahum wa 'itratahul aTaayeb

The praising of Allah (AJ) that embraces all of Prophet's holy family and his companions,
Also his descendants that are eternally blessed

CHORUS

اَللّهُمَّ صَلِّ وَ سَلِّمْ وَ بَارِكْ عَلَيْهِ وَ عَلَي أَلِهْ
Allahuma salli wa sallim wa barik 'alayhi wa 'ala alih
O Allah (AJ) send peace and blessings upon Prophet Muhammad (pbuh) and his family.

Ishfa'lana

اِشْفَعْ لَنَا

(اِشْفَعْ لَنَا، لَنَا نَا نَا، يَا حَبِيبَنَا) x٢

لَكَ شَفَاعَة   يَا رَسُوْلَ الله

يَا يَا نَبِيْ يَا نَبِيْ

يَا رَسُوْلَ الله   يَا يَا نَبِيْ، يَا نَبِيْ

(لَكَ شَفَاعَة   وَ هَذَا مَطْلَبِيْ، يَا نَبِيْ) x٢

(Ishfa'lana, lana na na, Ya Habibana) x2
Laka shafa'at, Ya Rasul Allah,
Ya Ya Nabi, Ya Nabi
Yaa Rasul Allah, Yaa Yaa Nabi, Yaa Nabi
Laka shafa'at, Wa Haza Math labbi, Yaa Nabi x2

Intercede for us, O our Beloved, You are gifted with Intercession,
O Messenger of Allah (AJ), O Prophet Muhammad (pbuh), You are gifted with
Intercession, and this is what I seek from you, O Prophet

اِشْفَعْ لَنَا يَا يَا، يَا خَيْرُ الْأَنَامْ x٢   أَنْتَ الْمُرْتَجَى، يَوْمَ الزِّحَامْ

Antal murtajaa, Yaumaz zihaam   Ishfa'lana Yaa, Yaa Khairul Anam x2

You are our only hope on the Day of Gathered Crowd (judgement Day), Intercede
for us O best of Mankind

CHORUS

أَنْتَ لِلْقَلْبِ يَا، يَا طَبِيْبُ x٢   لُذْنَا بِكَ يَا، يَا حَبِيْبُ

Luzna Bika Yaa, Yaa Habibu   Anta lil qalbi Yaa, Yaa Tabibu x2

You are our remedy, O beloved, you are the healer of our hearts

CHORUS

تَنْشُرُ الْهِدَايَة، بَيْنَ الْعَالَمِيْنِ x٢   جِئْتَ لِلْبَرَايَا، بِالشَّرْع الْمُبِيْن

Ji'ta lil baraya, bishar'il Mubeen   Tanshurul hidayah, bainal 'alamin x2

You came to creation with the clear divinely constitution, You spread guidance to the
worlds and took away ignorance

CHORUS

Allahu Rabbi, Rabbi Ta'ala

اللهُ رَبِّيْ، رَبِّيْ تَعَالَى

(يَا حَبِيْبِيْ صِلْنِيْ حَبِيْبِيْ فَالْعَهْدُ طَالَا) x۲   (اللهُ رَبِّيْ، رَبِّيْ تَعَالَى) x۲

(Allahu Rabbi, Rabbi Ta'ala) x2
(Ya Habibi silni habibi fal'ahdu Talaa) x2

Allah (AJ) is my Lord, my Lord All Mighty, O my Beloved connect me to my origin. My journey has been long and I am awaiting to return to You

---

(عِلْمَهُ بِحَالِيْ حَبِيْبِيْ يَكْفِي الْمَقَالَا) x۲   (دَعَوْتُ رَبِّيْ، وَالرَّبُّ يَعْلَمْ) x۲

(Da'awtu Rabbi, war rabbu ya'lam) x2
('ilmahu bihali Habibi yakfi maqala) x2

I prayed to my Lord and my Lord knows everything, O my Lord, you know my condition better than I could ever describe

CHORUS

(وَالآنَ صَبْرِيْ حَبِيْبِيْ، قَدْ سَاءَ حَالَا) x۲   (صَبَرْتُ صَبْرًا، حُلْوًا جَمِيْلًا) x۲

(Sabartu sabran, hulwan jamila) x2
(Wal aana sabri Habibi, qad sa'a hala) x2

I have patiently endured separation from You, my Beloved, and now I am running out of patience, have pity on my condition

CHORUS

(حِسًّا وَمَعْنَى حَبِيْبِيْ، حَالًا وَقَالَا) x۲   (حَبِيْبِيْ زُرْنِيْ، وَاَعْلِ شَأْنِيْ) x۲

(Habibi zurni, wa'ali shani) x2
(Hissan wa ma'na Habibi halan wa qala) x2

O my Beloved, gaze upon me and raise my station. Purify me physically and morally, improve my condition and how I speak to others

CHORUS

(قَرْبِيْ وَبُعْدِيْ، عِزِّيْ وَذُلِّيْ) x٢   (حُبَّكْ فَتَنِّي حَبِيْبِيْ، وَدَمْعِيْ سَالَا) x٢

(Qurbi wa bu'di, 'izzi wa dhulli) x2
(Hubbak fatanni Habibi wa dam'i sala) x2

My nearness and my distance from you, my dignity and my humility,
Your love enchanted me and my tears are flowing

CHORUS

(قَوْلُوْا جَمِيْعًا، صَلَاةَ رَبِّيْ) x٢   (عَلَى حَبِيْبِيْ مُحَمَّدْ، خَيْرِ الرِّجَالَا) x٢

(Qawlu jami'an, salatu rabbi) x2
('Ala Habibi-Muhammad, khairi rijala) x2

All of you say, O Lord bestow blessings upon my Beloved
Prophet Muhammad (pbuh), the best of men and mankind!

CHORUS

اَللّٰهُمَّ صَلِّ وَ سَلِّمْ وَ بَارِكْ عَلَيْهِ وَ عَلَي اَلِهْ
Allahuma salli wa sallim wa barik 'alayhi wa 'ala alih
O Allah (AJ) send peace and blessings upon Prophet Muhammad (pbuh) and his family.

Ayyuhal Mushtaq

أَيُّهَا الْمُشْتَاقُ

أَيُّهَا الْمُشْتَاقُ لَا تَنَم   هَذِهِ أَنْوَارُ ذِي سَلَم

عَنْ قَرِيبٍ أَنْتَ فِي الْحَرَم   عِنْدَ الْخَيْرِ الْعُرْبِ وَالْعَجَم

Ayyuhal mushtaqu la tanami   **Hadhihi anwaru dhi Salami**
An qaribin anta Fil Harami   **'Inda khayril 'urbi wal 'ajami**

O you who is in love and longs to see the beloved, Do not sleep, Ahead are the illuminated lights of Dhi Salam Valley, You are so close to the sacred sanctuary of Madina, In the presence of the One who is the best of the Arabs and non-Arabs

قِفْ أَمَامَ الْقَبْرِ فِي أَدَب   مَاثِلًا فِي أَشْرَفِ الرُّتُب

فِي مَكَانِ الْقُرْبِ وَالْقُرَب   وَالرِّضَا وَالْجُودِ وَالْكَرَم

Qif amamal qabri fi adabi   **Mathilan fi ashrafir rutabi**
Fi makanil qurbi wal qurabi   **Warrida wal jodi wal karami**

Stand in reverence in front of Prophet Muhammad's (pbuh) holy grave, You are in the presence of the one who has the most honourable ranks in Divine presence, In his resting place is the privilege of nearness to Him and Divine's satisfaction, contentment and generosity

CHORUS

ثُمَّ قُلْ يَا أَشْرَفِ الرُّسَل   يَا حَبِيبُ اللهِ فِي الْأَمَل

يَاعَظِيمُ الْعِلْمِ وَالْعَمَل   يَا سَمِيرُ اللَّوْحِ وَالْقَلَم

Thuma qul ya ashrafer Rusli   **Ya Habibullahi fil amali**
Ya 'Azimul 'ilmi wal 'amali   **Ya Samirul Lawhi wal Qalami**

Then say O honoured Messenger, O Beloved of Allah (AJ) who inspires hope, O Magnificent in your Knowledge and Action, O the one who speaks from the Reserved Tablet and the holy Pen.

CHORUS

فَهْوَ مِلْئُ السَّمْعِ وَالْبَصَرِ
وَإِمَامُ الرُّسْلِ وَالْأُمَمِ

لَيْسَ كَالْمُخْتَارِ فِي الْبَشَرِ
وَاحِدُ التَّارِيْخِ وَالسِّيَرِ

Laysa kal Mukhtari fil bashari
Wahidut tarikhi was siyari

Fahwa milus sam'yi wal basari
Wa Imamur Rusli wal Umami

No one from humanity can be compared to the Chosen One, Prophet Muhammad (pbuh), He exists in our hearing and sight. He is the unique one in the history and what is preceding. He is the leader of all the Messengers and all the nations.

CHORUS

وَعَلَى الْمِعْرَاجِ مَرْقَاهُوْ
بِكَلَامٍ لَيْسَ كَالْكَلِمِ

لَيْلَةَ الْإِسْرَاءِ تَرْعَاهُوْ
حَتَّى أَدْنَاهُوْ وُنَاجَاهُوْ

Lailatul Isra yi tar 'aahu
Hata Adna hu wa najahu

Wa 'alal Mi'raju mar qahu
Biklamin laysa kal kalimi

The Night of Journey safeguards him (Prophet Muhammad (pbuh)), And on his Ascension is his high rank, When Allah (AJ) brought him nearer (to the Divine Presence) and they conversed, With words unlike any other words

CHORUS

دُوْنَهَا كُلُّ الْوَرَى وُقِفُوْا
ثُمَّ أَوْ أَدْنَى إِلَى الْقِمَمِ

رُتْبَةَ مَا بَعْدَهَا شَرَفُ
قَابَ قَوْسَيْنِ لَهَا طَرَفُ

Rutbatun ma ba'daha sharafu
Qaba qawsayni laha tarafu

Dunaha kullul wara wuqifu
Summa aw adna ilal qimami

He reached the most honourable rank, that no one in God's creation could ever reach, As one end seemed to be within the Two bows' length or even closer to the Divine presence, And the other even further than the Sky

CHORUS

اَللَّهُمَّ صَلِّ وَ سَلِّمْ وَ بَارِكْ عَلَيْهِ وَ عَلَي آلِهْ
Allahuma salli wa sallim wa barik 'alayhi wa 'ala alih
O Allah (AJ) send peace and blessings upon Prophet Muhammad (pbuh) and his family.

Rabbi Faghfir li Dhunubi

رَبِّي فَأغْفِرْلِيْ ذِنُوْبِيْ

بِبَرْكَةِ الْهَادِيْ مُحَمَّدْ ، يَا الله | (رَبِّي فَأغْفِرْلِيْ ذِنُوْبِيْ، يَا الله)×٢

(Rabbi faghfir li dhunubi Ya Allah
Bi barkatil Hadi Muhammad Ya Allah) x2

O my Lord, forgive my sins, O Allah (AJ),
By the blessings of the Perfected guide, Prophet Muhammad (pbuh), O Allah (AJ)

فِيْ جِوَارِه خَيْرَ مَقْعَدْ، يَا الله | رَبِّي بَلِّغْنَا بِجَاهِهْ، يَا الله

Rabbi balighna bi jahi, ya Allah
Fi jiwari khayra maq'ad, ya Allah

O my Lord, let us reach (our destination), for the sake of Prophet Muhammad's (pbuh)
high station (with You), In his proximity is the best place to stay

CHORUS

أَشْرَفَ الرُّسْلِ مُحَمَّدْ، يَا الله | وَصَلَاةُ اللهِ تَغْشَى، يَا الله

Wa salatullahi taghsha, Ya Allah
Ashrafar Rusli Muhammad, Ya Allah

May Allah's (AJ) blessings shower him, Prophet Muhammad (pbuh) is the noblest of the
Messengers

CHORUS

كُلَّ حِيْنٍ يَا تَجَدَّدْ، يَا الله | وَسَلَامٌ مُسْتَمَرٌّ، يَا الله

Wa salamun mustamirrun, Ya Allah
Kulla hinin ya tajaddad, Ya Allah

Peace be upon him, Prophet Muhammad (pbuh), Continuously and renewed at every
moment

CHORUS

يَا رَسُوْلُ اللهِ أَهْلاً، يَا الله   بِكَ إِنَا بِكَ نُسْعَدْ، يَا الله

Ya Rasulullahi ahlan, Ya Allah
Bika inna bika nus'ad, Ya Allah

Welcome O Messenger of Allah (AJ) Welcome, For verily with you is our joy and happiness

CHORUS

وَ بِجَاهِهْ يَا إِلَهِيْ، يَا الله   جُدْ وَ بَلِّغْ كُلَّ مَقْصَدْ، يَا الله

Wa bijahi, ya ilahi, Ya Allah
Jud wa balligh kulla maqsad, Ya Allah

And by Prophet Muhammad's (pbuh) high honored station, O our Lord,
Give us generously and grant us all that we are in need of

CHORUS

وَاهْدِنَا نَهْجَ سَبِيْلِهْ، يَا الله   كَيْ بِهِ نُسْعَدْ وَنُرْشَدْ، يَا الله

Wahdina nahja sabilih, Ya Allah
Kay bihi nus'ad wa nurshad, Ya Allah

Guide us with his methods and directions, O Allah (AJ),
So that we receive happiness and guidance, O Allah (AJ)

CHORUS

اَللّهُمَّ صَلِ وَ سَلِّمْ وَ بَارِكْ عَلَيْهِ وَ عَلَي آلِهْ

Allahuma salli wa sallim wa barik 'alayhi wa 'ala alih

O Allah (AJ) send peace and blessings upon Prophet Muhammad (pbuh) and his family.

Salawat ul Badriyah
اَلصَّلَوَاتُ الْبَدْرِيَّة

عَلَى طٰهَ رَسُوْلِ الله
عَلَى يٰسَ حَبِيْبِ الله

صَلَاةُ الله، سَلَامُ الله
صَلَاةُ الله، سَلَامُ الله

Salatullah salamullah
Salatullah salamullah

'ala Taha Rasulillah
'ala Yaseen Habibillah

Allah's (AJ) praise and blessing is upon Taha (Purified Guide), Messenger of Allah (AJ).
Allah's (AJ) praise and blessing is upon the Yaseen, Beloved of Allah (pbuh)

وَ بِالْـهَادِى رَسُوْلِ الله
بِأَهْلِ الْبَدْرِ يَا الله

تَـوَسَّلْنَا بِبِسْمِ الله
وَ كُلِّ الْمُـجَاهِدِيْنْ لِلّٰهِ

Tawassalna bi Bismillah
Wa kullil mujahidin lillah

Wa bil Hadi Rasulillah
Bi ahlil badri ya Allah

Connect us by <u>means</u> of bismillah, And by the Perfected Guide, Messenger of Allah
(PBUH), And everyone who strives in Allah's (AJ) Way, By means of the family of the full
moon (Prophet Muhammad (pbuh)), O Allah (AJ)

CHORUS

مِنَ الْآفَاتِ وَالنَّقْمَة
بِأَهْلِ الْبَدْرِ يَا الله

إِلَهِي سَلِّمِ الْأُمَّة
وَمِنْ هَمٍّ وَمِنْ غُمَّه

Ilahi sallimil umma
Wa min hammin wa min ghummah

Minal aafati wan niqmah
Bi ahlil badri ya Allah

O my God, grant safety to the Nation, From diseases and retribution, And from worries
and from sadness, By means of the family of the full moon
(Prophet Muhammad (pbuh)),

CHORUS

جَمِيْعَ اَذِيَّةٍ وَا صْرِفْ
بِأَهْلِ الْبَدْرِ يَا الله

إِلَهِي نَجِّنَا وَاكْشِفْ
مَكَائِدَ الْعِدَا وَأَلْطَفْ

Ilahi najjina wakshif
Makaaidal 'idaa walTuf

Jami'a adhiyyatin wasrif
Bi ahlil badri ya Allah

My God, save us and lift all harm from us, and ward, Save us from our enemies'
schemes, By means of the family of the full moon (Prophet Muhammad (pbuh)),

CHORUS

مِنَ الْعَاصِيْنَ وَالْعَطْبَا | إِلَهِي نَفِّسِ الْكُرَبَة
بِأَهْلِ الْبَدْرِ يَا الله | وَ كُلِّ بَلِيَّةٍ وَوَبَاء

Ilahi naffisil kurbah
Wa kulla baliyyatin wa wabaa

Minal 'aasina wal 'atba
Bi ahlil badri ya Allah

My God, relieve us from the distress, From the disobedient and corrupt ego and save us from every trial and epidemic, By means of the family of the full moon (Prophet Muhammad (pbuh)), O Allah (AJ)

CHORUS

وَكَمْ مِنْ ذِلَّةٍ فَصَلَتْ | فَكَمْ مِنْ رَحْمَةٍ حَصَلَتْ
بِأَهْلِ الْبَدْرِ يَا الله | وَ كَمْ مِنْ نِعْمَةٍ وَصَلَتْ

Fakam min rahmatin hasalat
Wa kam min ni'matin wasalat

Wa kam min dhillatin fasalat
Bi ahlil badri ya Allah

How many mercies have occurred! And how many humiliations were lifted! How many favours have been granted! By means of the family of the full moon (Prophet Muhammad (pbuh)), O Allah (AJ)

CHORUS

وَكَمْ أَوْلَيْتَ ذَالْعُمْرِ | وَ كَمْ اَغْنَيْتَ ذَالْفَقْرِ
بِأَهْلِ الْبَدْرِ يَا الله | وَ كَمْ عَافَيْتَ ذَا الْوِزْرِ

Wa kam aghnayta dhal faqri
Wa kam 'afayta dhal wizri

Wa kam awlayta dhal 'umri
Bi ahlil badri ya Allah

How many poor people have You sustained! How many old people have You taken care of, How many burdens have you lifted from the helpless! By means of the family of the full moon (Prophet Muhammad (pbuh)), O Allah (AJ)

CHORUS

وَ جُلِّ الْخَيْرِ وَ السَّعْدِ | أَتَيْنَا طَالِبِى الرِّفْقِ
بِأَهْلِ الْبَدْرِ يَا الله | فَوَسِّعْ مِنْحَةَ الْأَيْدِئ

Atayna talibir rafqi
Fawassa' minhatal aydi

Wa julil khayri wassa'di
Bi ahlil badri ya Allah

We came here asking for your mercy, And for abundance of goodness and joy, So expand Your grants, By means of the family of the full moon (Prophet Muhammad (pbuh)), O Allah (AJ)

CHORUS

فَـلاَ تَرْدُدْ مَعَ الْخَيْبَة | بَلِ إجْعَلْنَا عَلَى الطَّيْبَة
أَيَـا ذَا الْعِـزِّ وَ الْهَـيْبَة | بِأَهْلِ الْبَدْرِ يَا الله

Fala tardud ma'al khayba   **Balij'alna 'alatTayba**
Aya dhal 'izza walhayba   **Bi ahlil badri ya Allah**

Don't turn us back disheartened, Rather let us achieve goodness, O Most Honoured
and full of Majesty, By means of the family of the full moon
(Prophet Muhammad (pbuh)), O Allah (AJ)

CHORUS

وَ إِنْ تَرْدُدْ فَمَنْ نَأْتِىْ | بِنَيْلِ جَمِيْعِ حَاجَا تِى
أَيَـا جَـالِى الْمُـلِـمَّـاتِ | بِأَهْلِ الْبَدْرِ يَا الله

Wa in tardud faman nati   **Binayli jami'e hajati**
Aya jalil mulimmati   **Bi ahlil badri ya Allah**

If You refuse us to whom shall we go, for all our needs? O the one who washes away all
hardships, By means of the family of the full moon
(Prophet Muhammad (pbuh)), O Allah (AJ)

CHORUS

اَللّهُمَّ صَلِ وَ سَلِّمْ وَ بَارِكْ عَلَيْهِ وَ عَلَي أَلِهْ
Allahuma salli wa sallim wa barik 'alayhi wa 'ala alih
O Allah (AJ) send peace and blessings upon Prophet Muhammad (pbuh) and his family.

Ahmad Ya Habibi

اَحْمَدْ يَا حَبِيْبِيْ

(اَحْمَدْ يَا حَبِيْبِيْ, سَلَّامْ عَلَيك) x ٤

(Ahmad Ya Habibi, Salaam 'Alayk) x4
O my beloved Ahmad (most praised), peace be upon you

مِنْ عِنْدِ الرَّحْمَنِ، سَلَّامْ عَلَيك   جِئْتَ بِالْقُرَآنِ، سَلَّامْ عَلَيك

جِئْتَ بِالْقُرَآنِ، مِنْ عِنْدِ الرَّحْمَنِ، سَلَّامْ عَلَيك

Jita bil Qurani, Salaam 'Alayk   Min 'indir Rahmani, Salaam 'Alayk

Jita bil Qurani, Min 'indir Rahmani, Salaam 'Alayk

You came with holy Quran, From the most Merciful, Peace be upon you,

CHORUS

يَا حَبِيْبَ اللهِ، سَلَّامْ عَلَيك   يَا رَسُولَ اللهِ، سَلَّامْ عَلَيك

يَارَسُولَ اللهِ، يَا حَبِيْبَ اللهِ، سَلَّامْ عَلَيك

Ya RasulAllahi, Salaam 'Alayk   Ya HabibAllahi, Salaam 'Alayk

Ya RasulAllahi, Ya HabibAllahi, Salaam 'Alayk

O Messenger of Allah (AJ), O Beloved of Allah (AJ), Peace be upon you

CHORUS

يَا مَاحِي الذِّنُوْب ، سَلَّامْ عَلَيك   يَا مُحْيِي الْقُلُوْب، سَلَّامْ عَلَيك

يَا مُحْيِي الْقُلُوْب، يَا مَاحِي الذِّنُوْبِ ، سَلَّامْ عَلَيك

Ya Muhyil qulubi, Salaam 'Alayk   Ya Mahidh dhunubi, Salaam 'Alayk

Ya Muhyil qulubi, Ya Mahidh dhunubi, Salaam 'Alayk

O the reviver of the hearts, O the eraser of the sins, Peace be upon you

CHORUS

يَا أَبَا الْقَاسِمِ، سَلَامْ عَلَيك   يا أَبَا الزَّهْرَاءِ ، سَلَامْ عَلَيك

يَا أَبَا الْقَاسِمِ ، يا أَبَا الزَّهْرَاءِ ، سَلَامْ عَلَيك

Ya abul Qaasemi, Salaam 'Alayk   Ya abaz Zahraaye, Salaam 'Alayk

Ya abul Qaasemi, Ya abaz Zahraahi, Salaam 'Alayk

O father of Qasim (as), O father of Fatima Zahra (as), Peace be upon you

CHORUS

يَا جَدَّ الْحَسَّنِ ، سَلَامْ عَلَيك   يَا جَدَ الْحُسَّيْن ، سَلَامْ عَلَيك

يَا جَدَ الْحَسَّنِ، يَا جَدَ الْحُسَّيْنِ ، سَلَامْ عَلَيك

Ya Jaddal Hassani Salaam 'Alayk   Ya Jaddal Hussaini Salaam 'Alayk

Ya Jaddal Hassani, Ya Jaddal Hussaini, Salaam 'Alayk

O grandfather of Imam Hassan (as), O grandfather of Imam Hussain (as), Peace be upon you

CHORUS

اَللهُمَّ صَلِ وَ سَلِّمْ وَ بَارِكْ عَلَيْهِ وَ عَلَى اَلِهْ

Allahuma salli wa sallim wa barik 'alayhi wa 'ala alih

O Allah (AJ) send peace and blessings upon Prophet Muhammad (pbuh) and his family.

AnNabi Sallu 'Alayh

اَلنَّبِيْ صَلُوْا عَلَيْهِ

اَلنَّبِيْ صَلُوْا عَلَيْهِ
وَيَنَالُ الْبَرَكَة

صَلَوَاتُ الله عَلَيْهِ
كُلُّ مَنْ صَلَى عَلَيْهِ

Salawatullah 'alayh
Kullu man salla 'alayh

AnNabi sallu 'alayh
Wa yanalul Barakah

Praise the Prophet Muhammad (pbuh)! Allah (AJ) bestowed blessings upon Him,
And everyone who praises Him, Will be granted blessings from Allah (AJ)

(اَلنَّبِيْ يَا مَنْ حَضَر
مَنْ لَهُ شَقَّ الْقَمَر

اَلنَّبِيْ خَيْرُ الْبَشَر) x٢
وَالْغَزَالْ سَلّمْ عَلَيْه

AnNabi khayrul bashar) x2
Wal ghazal Sallam 'alayh

(AnNabi ya man hadar
Man lahu shaqqal qamar

He is the Prophet (pbuh); O attendees, The Prophet (Muhammad (pbuh)) is the best
of creation! He split the moon, and the gazelle (deer) and all creation greeted Him

CHORUS

(اَلنَّبِيْ ذَاكَ الْعَرُوس
اَلنَّصَارَى وَالْمَجُوس

ذِكْرُهِ يُحِي النَّفُوس) x٢
أَسْلَمُوْا عَلَى يَدَيْهِ

Dhikru hee yuhen nufus) x2
Aslamu 'ala yaday

(AnNabi Dhakal 'arus
Annasara wal Majus

The Prophet (pbuh) is the most beloved to the Divine, His remembrance and praise
revives the souls, the Christians and Magi (Zoroastrian priests), accepted Islam by his
hands

CHORUS

(اَلنَّبِيْ ذَاكَ الْمَلِيح
وَالْقُرَآنْ شَيْءٌ صَحِيح

قَوْلُهُ قَوْلٌ فَصِيحْ) x٢
اَلَذِيْ أَنْزِلْ عَلَيْه

Qawluhu qawlun fasih) x2
Alladhi unzil 'alayh

(AnNabi Dhakal malih
Wal Qur'an shayun sahih

The Prophet is sweet, is pleasant and he has excellent character, His words are eloquent,
And Holy Quran, the uncreated words of Allah (AJ), is an absolute truth, That was
revealed to Him

CHORUS

اَعْلَمُوْا عِلْمَ الْيَقِيْنْ x۲
اَفْرَضَ الصَّلاةَ عَلَيْهْ

(اَلنَّبِيْ يَا حَاضِرِيْنْ
اَنَّ رَبَّ الْعَالَمِيْنَ

(AnNabi ya hadirin
Ana rabbal 'alamin

A'alamu 'ilmal yaqeen) x2
Afradas salat 'alay

The Prophet Muhammad (pbuh), O attendees, You should know this with certainty,
That the Lord of both worlds, made praising him, an obligation to creation

CHORUS

اَلَّذِيْ نُزَلْ قُبَا x۲
كُلُّكُمْ صَلُّو عَلَيْهْ

(اَلنَّبِيُّ الْمُجْتَبَي
اَظْهَرَ الدِّيْنِ وَ النَّبَا

(AnNabiyul Mujtaba
Azharaddin wanNaba

Alladhi nazal quba) x2
Kullukum sallu 'alayh

The Prophet, the chosen One, who passed by Quba (Qab Qawsayn, two bow arrows or
nearer), the Divine religion and prophecy was manifested and revealed by him, You all
praise Him

CHORUS

ابْنُ عَمِّ الرَّسُوْل x۲
وَالِإ لَهْ يَرْضَى عَلَيْهْ

(وَامْتَدِحْ زَوْجَ الْبَتُوْل
مَنْ اَحَبْهُمْ فِيْ قَبُوْل

(Wamtadih zawjal batul
Man ahabhum fi qabul

Ibnu 'ammi li Rasul) x2
Wal ilah yarda 'alayh

And praise husband of (Perfected Light) Fatima (Imam Ali (as)) the Prophet's cousin,
Whoever loves Prophet's family (Ahlul Bayt), Allah (AJ) is pleased with them

CHORUS

لِلنَّبِيْ قَرَّةَ عَيْن x۲
جَدُّهُمْ صَلُّو عَلَيْهْ

(اَلْحَسَنْ ثُمَ الْحُسَيْن
نُوْرُهُمْ كَالْكَوْكَبَيْن

(Al Hassan thumal Husayn
Nooruhum kal kawkabayn

Lin Nabi qurratu 'ayn) x2
Jadduhum sallu 'alayh

Imam Hassan (as) then Imam Hussain (as), are very dear to Prophet (pbuh). They are the
coolness of his eyes, Their lights are like two bright stars, praise their Grandfather
(Muhammad (pbuh))

CHORUS

نُوْرُهُمْ يَعْلُ الْقَمَرْ) x٢
وَالإِ لَهْ يَسْخَطْ عَلَيْهِ

أَبُوْبكَرٍ وَ عُمَرْ)
مَنْ اَبْغَضْهُمْ فِيْ سَقَرْ

(Abu Bakrin wa 'Umar
Mana ab ghadhum fi saqar

Nooruhum ya'lul qamar) x2
Wal ilah yas khat 'alayh

The holy companions of Prophet (pbuh), Abu Bakr (as) and Umar (as), their light surpasses the moon, The one who hates them is in hell, And God is angry with him

CHORUS

مَنْ تَزَوَّجْ قَمَرَيْن) x٢
وَالْمَوْلَا يَرْضَى عَلَيْهِ

وَ تَرَضَا عَنْ ذِيْ النُّوْرَيْن)
مَنْ تَرَدَّا فِيْ خَيْرَيْن

(Wa tarada an ze-noorayn
Man tarada fi khay-rayn

Man tazawaj qamarayn) x2
Wa Mawla yarda 'alayh

And Allah (AJ) is pleased with the beholder of two lights (Othman (as)), who married the two moons (daughters of the Prophet (pbuh)), Who received two sources of lights. And the Lord is pleased with him.

CHORUS

اَللّهُمَّ صَلِ وَ سَلِّمْ وَ بَارِكْ عَلَيْهِ وَ عَلَيْ آلِهْ
Allahuma salli wa sallim wa barik 'alayhi wa 'ala alih
O Allah (AJ) send peace and blessings upon Prophet Muhammad (pbuh) and his family.

Nahran min Laban

نَهْرًا مِنْ لَبَنْ

(إِنَّ فِي الْجَنَّةِ نَهْرًا مِنْ لَبَنْ   لِعَلِيٍّ وَ حُسَيْنٍ وَ حَسَنْ) ×٢

(Inna fil jannati nahran min laban   **Li 'Aliyin wa Hussainin wa Hassan) x2**

In heaven there is a river of Milk for Imam 'Ali (as), and Imam Hussain (as),
and Imam Hassan (as)

يَا رَسُولاً، قَدْ حَبَانَا حُبُّهُ فَضْلاً وَ مَنْ   (جُدْ عَلَيْنَا بِالتَّجَلِّي، نَرْتَجِيْ مِنْكَ الْمِنَنْ) ×٢

Ya Rasulan, qad habana, hubbuhu fadlan wa man
(Jud 'alayna bittajali, nartaji minkal minan) x2

O Messenger of Allah (AJ), your love has rewarded us with favours and grants,
Be generous to us with your manifestation, we seek from you your lights and realities

CHORUS

جِئْتُ شَوْقًا وَغَرَامًا، فِي هَوَا قَلْبِي حَسَنْ   (رَاجِياً مِنْهُ اِبْتِسَامًا، مَنْ لَهُ رُوْحِيْ ثَمَنْ) ×٢

Jitu shawqan, wa gharaaman, fi hawa qalbi Hassan
(Rajiyan minhub tisaman, man lahu ruhi thaman) x2

I came full of love and yearning, and my heart full of desire to be close to you,
I will present my soul to you for a gaze and smile from you

CHORUS

مِنْ فَوَادِيْ وَحَنِيْنِيْ وَحَنِينْ قَلْبِيْ وَ عَنْ   (وَرَأَى الطَّيْرُ حَنِيْنِيْ، تَبْكِيْ عَطْفًا وَعَنْ) ×٢

Min fuaadi, wa hanini, wa hanin qalbi wa 'an
(Wara a' Tayru hanini, tabki 'atfan wa 'an) x2

From the yearning of my heart and its moaning for you,
The birds saw my yearning, and started to cry in sympathy

CHORUS

وَ صَلَاتِيْ وَ سَلَامِيْ لِلنَّبِيِّ الْمُؤْتَمَنْ   (رَاجِياً حُسْنَ الْخِتَامِ بِالْحُسَيْنِ وَالْحَسَنْ) ×٢

WaSsalati, wa salami, linNabiyyil mutaman
(Rajiyan husnal khitami, bil Hussaini wal Hassan) x2

Praising and blessings be upon the trusted Prophet Muhammad (pbuh), We
pray to have a good ending by the means of Imam Hussain (as) and Imam Hassan (as)

CHORUS

Nadi Ali (as)

نَادِعَلِيْ (ع)

(نَادِ عَلِياً مُظْهَرُ العَجَائِب   تَجِدْهُ عَوْنَا لَكَ فِي النَّوَائِب) ٢x

عَلِي عَلِي عَلِي عَلِي، يَا عَلِي

عَلِي عَلِي عَلِي عَلِي، يَا عَلِي

(Nadi Aliyan Muzharul 'ajayeb

Tajidhu 'awnallaka fin nawayeb) x2

(Ali, Ali, Ali, Ali, Ya Ali) x2

Call upon Imam Ali (as) who manifests wondrous appearances,
He will rescue and support you in times of difficulties and calamities

سُبْحَانْ رَبِّي ا لْصَاغْ لَكَ هَالْإِسْمْ، يَا عَلِي   يَا عَلِي إِسْمَكْ بِالْقَلْبِ مِنْرِسِمْ، يَا عَلِي

ثَغْرِالْمَوْدَةِ بِمَوْلَدَكْ مِبْتِسِمْ ، يَا عَلِي   يَا مَنْبَعِ الْجُوْدِ وُكِنُوزِالْعِلِمْ، يَا عَلِي

عَنْ قَلْبْ صَادِقْ بِالْعَدِلْ مِعْتِصِمْ، يَا عَلِي   آخِرَوْدُنْيَا بْمِنْهَجَكْ نِلْتِزِمْ، يَا عَلِي

(أَنْتَ لِوَاءُ الْفَخْرِ وَالْمَنَاقِبْ

وَجَوْهَرُالْعِزَّةِ وَالْمَوَاهِبْ) ٢x

(عَلِي عَلِي عَلِي عَلِي، يَا عَلِي) ٢x

Ya Ali Ismak, bilqalb min risem, YA ALI
Subahan Rabbil, saghlak hal isem, YA ALI
Ya Man-ba'al judu, keno'zil 'ilem, YA ALI
Thaghril maw'adat, bemawlidak mibtisem, YA ALI
Akhiraw Dunyabe menhajak 'niltizem, YA ALI
An Qaleb Sadiq, bil 'adil mi'etisem, YA ALI

(Anta Liwaul Fakhri wal Manaqeb
Wa Jawharul 'Izzati wal Mawaheb) x2
(Ali, Ali, Ali, Ali, Ya Ali) x2

O Ali (as) your name is engraved on my heart, Glory be to my Lord who gave you that name "Ali" (the Most High), From Prophet's (pbuh) ocean, you are the manifestation of generosity and the treasure, The Prophet (pbuh) is the city of all knowledges and you are the door, The holy lips of Prophet Muhammad (pbuh) smiled with love at your birth and arrival, In here and hereafter the saints have pledged their allegiance to faithfully follow the path of love, From a truthful heart we hold tight to your justice and authority, Your banner is our pride and Honour and you are the example of chivalry and moral excellence, From Prophet (pbuh) flows the essence of Power and Strength to you

CHORUS

أَشْرَفْ إِسْمْ فَوْقَ الضَّمِيرْ إِنْكِتَبْ، يَا عَلِي   أَسْمَكْ وُفَضْلَكْ نَالْ أَعْلَى الْرُّتَبْ، يَا عَلِي

مَا يَوْمْ نُورَكْ يَا بُوْحُسْنِينْ إِنْحَجَبْ، يَا عَلِي   هَالْفَضْلْ بَارِيْنَا لُوْجُودَكْ وَهَبْ، يَا عَلِي

كُلِ الْوُجُودْ تِّرَابْ وَأَنْتَ الذَّهَبْ، يَا عَلِي   حُبَّكْ فَرِيضَة وَّبِالشَّرَايِعْ وِجَبْ، يَا عَلِي

(شَأْنَكَ فَوْقَ الشَّأْنِ وَالْمَرَاتِبْ

يَا بُلْغَةَ الْإِحْسَانِ وَالْمَكَاسِبْ) x٢

(عَلِي عَلِي عَلِي عَلِي، يَا عَلِي) x٢

Ashraf Isem, fau'qaz zamir inkitab, YA ALI
Ismaku fadhlak, naal a`alar rutab, YA ALI
Ma yawm Nurak, Ya Bu Hussnein, inhajab, YA ALI
Hal fadel Barinal wojudak wahab, YA ALI
Kulil wojudit Tarab, wa Antaz Zahab, YA ALI
Hubbuk Faridau bishraa`i wejab, YA ALI

**(Sha'anuka fauqash Sha'ani wal Maratib
Ya Bulghatal Ihsani wal Makasib) x2
Ali, Ali, Ali, Ali, Ya Ali x2**

The honourable name of Imam Ali (as) is inscribed upon the heart and upon the conscience, Your name and grace has reached the highest ranks, O father of Imam Hassan (as) and Imam Hussain (as), your light has never been veiled from the world, God has given this Honour to your existence. Everything else is but a dust and you are the Gold, O Imam Ali (as), your love is an obligation and mandatory. Your lofty position is above all the stations and ranks of Saints, You have reached the station of excellence and high achievements

CHORUS

بِوُجُودَكْ الدِّيْن الْحَنِيفْ إِنْوَجَدْ، يَا عَلِي   لِلْكَوْن إِنْتَ السُّورْ وَإِنْتَ الْعَمَدْ، يَا عَلِي

وِبِزُودَكْ الْخَالِقْ يَا حَيْدَرْ شَهَدْ، يَا عَلِي   يَاأَسَدْ غَالِبْ مَا شَبِيهَكْ أَسَدْ، يَا عَلِي

لَا مَالْ يِنْفَعْ لَا أَهِلْ لَا وَلَدْ، يَا عَلِي   بِالْحَشِرْ بَسْ حُبَّكْ يَا حَيْدَرْسَنَدْ، يَا عَلِي

(يَوْمَ ظُهُورِ الْفَضْل وَالْمَثَالِبْ

لَا يَنْفَعُ الْأَدْنَى مِنَ الْأَقَارِبْ) x٢

(عَلِي عَلِي عَلِي عَلِي، يَا عَلِي) x٢

Lilkaun intas soor, wa Intal 'amad, YA ALI
Biwujudak dinil hanifin wijad, YA ALI
Ya Assad Ghalib, ma shabihak Assad, YA ALI
Wibzudak Khaliq, Ya Haidar Shahad, YA ALI
Bilhashr bas Hubbak Ya Haidar Sanad, YA ALI
La mal yinfa' la ahil la walad, YA ALI

(Yawma Zuhoril Fadhli wal Mathalib
La yanfa'ul adna minal Aqarib) x2
(Ali, Ali, Ali, Ali, Ya Ali) x2

You guard the universe; you are the pillar of strength. Through your reality, the perfect religion (Islam) has continued to exist. O the victorious lion, no lion resembles you. By your greatness, the creator has testified. In the Day of Judgment the love of Prophet (pbuh), Ahlul Bayt, Sahabi, and Saints, is enough for me. In the day when all the good and bad is apparent, Not wealth, nor family, nor relatives would be of any help or benefit.

CHORUS

اَللّٰهُمَّ صَلِّ وَ سَلِّمْ وَ بَارِكْ عَلَيْهِ وَ عَلَي اَلِهْ

Allahuma salli wa sallim wa barik 'alayhi wa 'ala alih

O Allah (AJ) send peace and blessings upon Prophet Muhammad (pbuh) and his family.

Part B

Maa Lanaa Mawlan Siwallah

مَالَنَا مَوْلًا سِوَى الله

الله الله , الله الله
كُلَّمَا نَادَيْتَ يَاهُو

مَالَنَا مَوْلًا سِوَى الله
قَالَ يَاعَبْدِئ أَنَا الله

Allah Allah, Allah Allah
Kulla maa naa daita yaa Hu

Maa lanaa mawlan siwallah
Qala ya 'abdi anAllah

O Allah (AJ), there is no God but Allah (AJ). Whenever I call out O my Lord, "O Hu." He says: "O my servant, I am Allah (AJ)."

وَأَتَى النّصْرُ مِنَ الله
وَشَرِيْفُ كَرَّمَ الله

فِي رَبِيْعٍ أَطْلَعَ الله
يَا لَهُ شَهْرُ عَظِيْمُ

Fi Rabi'in, atla' Allah
Ya lahu shahru 'Azimu

Wa atan nasru minAllah
Wa sharifu karramAllah

In Rabi' (Awwal) Allah (AJ) announced the arrival of Prophet Muhammad (pbuh); And He granted us victory through him, What a great month! Allah (AJ) conferred honour to His noble Servant

CHORUS

وَبِنَيْلِ الْقَصْدِ فُزْنَا
وَعَلَيْنَا أَنْعَمَ الله

فِيْهِ جَمْعًا قَدْ فَرِحْنَا
يَا رَسُوْلَ اللهِ طِبْنَا

Fihi jam'an, qad farihna
Ya RasulAllahi Tibna

Wa benaylil qasdi fuzna
Wa 'alayna an'amAllah

All of us take immense pleasure in this month, And we fulfilled our intention, O Messenger of Allah (AJ), we have the utmost delight, as Allah (AJ) bestowed His blessing upon us and sent you as a mercy to creation

CHORUS

بِظُهُوْرِ الْهَادِي اَحْمَدْ
ذَلِكَ الْفَضْلُ مِنَ اللّٰه

ظَهَرَ الدِّيْنُ الْمُؤَيَّدْ
يَاهَنَّانَا بِمُحَمَّدْ

Zahara ddin ul mu'ayyad
Ya hanana bi Muhammad

Bi zuhuril Hadi Ahmad
Dhalikal Fadhlu minAllah

Allah's (AJ) eternal religion manifested, by the arrival and birth of the Perfected Guide, Prophet Ahmad (pbuh). Our peace and joy can only be achieved by the presence of Prophet Muhammad (pbuh) whom is the grace and bounty of Allah (AJ)

CHORUS

كَانَ مِيْلَادُ الشَّفِيْع
مَنْ لَهُ قَدْ اَيَّدَ الله

ثَانِيْ عَشَرَ فِيْ رَبِيْع
صَاحِبُ الْقَدْرِ الرَّفِيْع

Thani 'ashri fi Rabi'yin
Sahibul Qadrir Rafi'yin

Kana Miladush Shafi'yi
Man lahu qad ayadAllah

On the twelfth of Rabi' ul Awwal, the intercessor (Muhammad (pbuh)) was born, The owner of supreme power and highest rank, He is Allah's (AJ) support and through him we achieve salvation

CHORUS

خَاتَمِ الرُّسْلِ الْكِرَام
وَأَتَى النَّصْرُ مِنَ الله

يَوْمَ مِيْلَادُ التَّهَامِيْ
زُخْرِفَتْ دَارُ السَّلَام

Yawma miladut tihami
Zukhrifat darus salami

Khatamir Ruslil kirami
Wa Atan nasru minAllah

On the birthday of the Prophet Muhammad (pbuh) from Tihama, The Seal of the Messengers, All the heavens were decorated and He is the Victory that Allah (AJ) sent us

CHORUS

اَللّٰهُمَّ صَلِّ وَ سَلِّمْ وَ بَارِكْ عَلَيْهِ وَ عَلَي اَلِهْ
Allahuma salli wa sallim wa barik 'alayhi wa 'ala alih
O Allah (AJ) send peace and blessings upon Prophet Muhammad (pbuh) and his family.

Salawat Adnani

صَلَوَاتِ عَدْنَانِ

صَلَّى عَلَيْكَ اللهُ يَا عَدْنَانِ
اَلْحَمْدُ لِلَّهِ الَّذِي أَعْطَانِيْ

يَا مُصْطَفَى يَا صَفْوَةَ الرَّحْمَانِ
(هَذَا الْغُلَامَ الطَّيِّبَ الْأَرْدَانِ) ٢x

Salla 'Alaik Alla'hu ya 'Adnani
Ya Mustafa Ya saf-watar Rahmani
Alhamdulilla'hil lazi a'tani
(Hazzaal ghulamat Thayy'ibal ardani) x2

May Allah's (AJ) blessings be upon you O descendant of Adnan, O Mustafa (Chosen One), the choice of the Most Merciful, we are grateful to Allah (AJ) for granting us, This pure boy who surpassed all his peers while still in the cradle

---

Qad saada fil Mahdi, 'alal ghelmani
U`idhuHu bil bayti zil'arkani
Hatta ara Hu balighal bunyani
(Anta'l ladhi summita fil Quraani) x2

قَدْ سَادَ فِى الْمَهْدِ، عَلَى الْغِلْمَانِ
أَعِيذُهُ بِالْبَيْتِ، ذِي الْأَرْكَانِ
حَتَّى أَرَاهُ بَالِغَ الْبُنْيَانِ
(أَنْتَ الَّذِي سُمِّيْتَ فِي الْقُرَآنِ) ٢x

Allah (AJ) protected him by the House (Ka'aba) with the strong corners, Until he reached manhood, O Prophet Muhammad (pbuh), you are the one whose name is mentioned in the Quran

CHORUS

Ahmad du'maktubun 'alal jinani
Salla 'alayk Allah hu' fil ahyani
Ahmad'duhu fis sirri wal burhani
(Haqqan 'alal Islami wal Imani) x2

أَحْمَدُ مَكْتُوْبٌ، عَلَى الْجِنَانِ
صَلَّى عَلَيْكَ اللهُ فِي الْأَحْيَانِ
أَحْمَدُهُ فِي السِّرِّ وَالْبُرْهَانِ
(حَقّاً عَلَى الْإِسْلَامِ وَالْإِيمَانِ) ٢x

Ahmad (Prophet Muhammad (pbuh)), whose name is written all over the walls of paradise, May Allah (AJ) shower His blessings upon you, Ahmad (saws), whom I praise loudly and in private, Is Truthful in his Islam (submission) and his Iman (faith)

CHORUS

Ahmad'duhu fis' sirri wal burhani

Haqqan 'alal Islami wal Imani

Ya rabbana bil Mustafal `Adnani

(Ighfir dhunubi' thumma asleh shani) x2

أَحْمَدُهُ فِي السِّرِّ وَالْبُرْهَانِ

حَقّاً عَلَى الْإِسْلَامِ وَالْإِيْمَانِ

يَا رَبَّنَا بِالْمُصْطَفَى الْعَدْنَانِ

(إِغْفِرْ ذُنُوْبِيْ ثُمَّ أَصْلِحْ شَأْنِيْ) ٢x

Ahmad, whom I praise loudly and in private, He is Truthful in Islam and Iman (faith), O Lord, by the Chosen One, the descendant of Adnan, Forgive my sins and give me good character

CHORUS

اَللّهُمَّ صَلِّ وَ سَلِّمْ وَ بَارِكْ عَلَيْهِ وَ عَلَي آلِهْ

Allahuma salli wa sallim wa barik 'alayhi wa 'ala alih

O Allah (AJ) send peace and blessings upon Prophet Muhammad (pbuh) and his family.

Tala'al Badru 'Alayna
طَلَعَ الْبَدْرُ عَلَيْنَا

طَلَعَ الْبَدْرُ عَلَيْنَا
وَجَبَ الشُّكْرُ عَلَيْنَا

مِنْ ثَنِيَاتِ الْوَدَاعْ
مَا دَعَا لِلّٰهِ دَاعْ

Tala'al badru 'alayna
Wa jabash shukuru 'alayna

Min thaniyatil wada'
Ma da'aa lillahi da'

O the full moon rose above us, From the valley of Wada',
Gratitude is our obligation, as long as anyone calls to Allah (AJ) for help

أَيُّهَا الْمَبْعُوثُ فِينَا
كُنْ شَفِيْعًا يَا حَبِيْبِيْ

جِئْتَ بِالْأَمْرِ الْمُطَاعْ
يَوْمَ حَشْرٍ وَاجْتِمَاعْ

Ayyuhal mab'uthu fina
Kun shafiy'an ya habibi

Jita bil amril muta'
Yawma hashrin wajtima'

O you who were sent among us, You came with Allah's (AJ) orders to be obeyed,
Intercede for us O our beloved, On the Day of gathering and judgement

CHORUS

رَبَّنَا صَلِّ عَلَي مَنْ
أَنْتَ غَوْثُنَا جَمِيْعًا

حَلَّ فِيْ خَيْرِ الْبِقَاعْ
يَا مُجَمَّلَ الطِّبَاعْ

Rabbana salli 'ala man
Anta ghawthuna jami'an

Halla fi khayrul biqa'
Ya mujammalat tiba'

O our Lord, send Your blessings upon the one, Who appeared in the best of all places,
You are our saviour (Prophet Muhammad (pbuh)), O the one who has the best of
characters

CHORUS

وَلَبِسْنَا ثَوْبَ عِزٍّ
أَسْبِلِ السِّتْرَ عَلَيْنَا

بَعْدَ تَلْفِيْقِ الرِقَاعْ
يَا مُجِيْبًا كُلَّ دَاعْ

Wa labisna thawba 'izzin
Asbili s'sitra 'alayna

Ba'da talfiqi riqa'
Ya mujiban kulla da'

We were adorned with the robe of honour, after patches and tatters
Cover our shortcomings, O the one who accepts all prayers

CHORUS

عَدَّدَ تَحْرِيرِ الرِّقَاعْ

وَصَلَاةُ الله عَلَى أَحْمَدْ

مَا سَعَا لِلّهِ سَاعْ

وَكَذَا آلٍ وَصَحْبٍ

Wa salatullah 'ala Ahmad
Wa kadha aalin wa sahbin

'adada tahriri riqa'
Ma sa'a lillahi sa'

And Allah's (AJ) blessing be upon Ahmad (pbuh), On the numbers of the freed lands,
likewise upon his Family and his Companions, as long as the striving is for Allah (AJ)

CHORUS

اَلَّلهُمَّ صَلِّ وَ سَلِّمْ وَ بَارِكْ عَلَيْهِ وَ عَلَي أَلِهْ
Allahuma salli wa sallim wa barik 'alayhi wa 'ala alih
O Allah (AJ) send peace and blessings upon Prophet Muhammad (pbuh) and his family.

Ya Gharami

يَاغَرَامِی

(صَلَاةً   بِالسَّلَامِ الْـمُبِينِ

لِنُقْطَةِ التَّعِيِينِ   يَاغَرَامِئْ) x۲

(Salatun,   bisSalamil mubini

Li nuqTatit ta'yini,   Ya gharami) x2

Blessings, and infinite peace be upon the one who is the point of origin and the source of all realities (Prophet Muhammad (pbuh)), O our Beloved

(نَبِيٌّ كَانَ ، أَصلَ التَّكوِينِ   مِنْ عَهْدِ كُنْ فَيَكُوْنُ يَاغَرَامِی) ۲x

(Nabiyun kaana, aslat takweeni

Min 'ahdi kun fayakun yaa gharami) x2

The Prophet (Muhammad (pbuh)) is the essence and source of creation, Since the time of the original promise of souls, and the saying "Kun fayaKun" (Be and it is)

CHORUS

(أَيَا مَن جَاءَنَا ، حَقًّا نَذِيرِ   مُغِيثًا مُسبِلاً ، سُبُلَ الرَّشَادِ) ۲x

(Aya manja-ana, haqqan nadhiri

Mughithan musbilan, subular rashadi) x2

O the one who came to us as a true warner (Prophet Muhammad (pbuh)), Our Saviour and Perfected Guide who has guided us to the right path and consciousness (taqwa)

CHORUS

(الله ،   يا الله،   يا الله،   يا الله) ۲x

(Allahhhh, Ya Allahhh, Ya Allahhh, Ya Allahhh) x2

(رَسُولُ اللهِ يَا، ضَاوِي الْجَبِينِ وَيَامَنْ جَآءَ بِالْحَقّ الْمُبِيْن)x٢

(Rasulullahi yaa, dawil jabini
Wayaa man ja'a bil haqqil mubini) x2

O Messenger of Allah (Prophet Muhammad (pbuh)), the bright light of your forehead is the sun that has illuminated the universes, You came with an absolute truth

CHORUS

(صَلَاةً لَمْ تَزَلْ، تُتْلَى عَلَيْكَ كَمِعْطَارِ النّسِيْم، تُهْدَى إِلَيْكَ) x٢

(Salatu lam tazal, tutla 'alayka
Kami'tarin nasim, Tuhda ilayka) x2

Blessings are sent upon you by Allah (AJ) and his angels, The whole creation, like a beautiful fragrance of the breeze , is given to you as a gift

CHORUS

اَلَّلهُمَّ صَلِ وَ سَلِّمْ وَ بَارِكْ عَلَيْهِ وَ عَلَي أَلِهْ
Allahuma salli wa sallim wa barik 'alayhi wa 'ala alih
O Allah (AJ) send peace and blessings upon Prophet Muhammad (pbuh) and his family.

Noor ul Mustafa

نُوْرُ الْمُصْطَفَي

Noorul Mustafaa, Noorul Mustafa

نُوْرُ الْمُصْطَفَي، نُوْرُ الْمُصْطَفَي

Mala alakwan, Mala alakwan

مَلَأَ الْأَكْوَانْ، مَلَأَ الْأَكْوَانْ

Habibi Muhammad, Muhammad,
Muhaaammad

حَبِيْبِيْ مُحَمَّدْ مُحَمَّدْ مُحَمَّدْ

Khayrul Mursaleen

خَيْرُ الْمُرْسَلِيْن

Light of Mustafa (Chosen One),Fills and illuminates the universes, My Beloved,
Muhammad, Muhammad, Muhammad, The Best of Messengers

(Allah dhul Jalal, a'takal Jamal) x2

(اَلله ذُوالْجَلَالْ، أَعْطَاكَ الْجَمَالْ) x٢

Ya Shamsal kamal, Ya noorul 'ayni

يَا شَمْسَ الْكَمَالْ، يَا نُوْرُ الْعَيْنِ

Habibi Muhammad, Muhammad,
Muhaaammad

حَبِيْبِيْ مُحَمَّدْ مُحَمَّدْ مُحَمَّدْ

Khayrul Mursaleen

خَيْرُ الْمُرْسَلِيْن

Allah (AJ), the Lord of Majesty, granted you heavenly beauty, O Sun of Perfection, O
light of my eyes/vision, My Beloved, Muhammad (pbuh), the Best of messengers.

CHORUS

(Nooru kal wadaah, Malik al arwah) x2

(نُوْرُكَ الْوَضَاحْ، مَالِكَ الْأَرْوَاحْ) x٢

Kam muhib bin rah, Il'al Hara'mayni

كَمْ مُحِبٍّ رَاحْ، إِلَي الْحَرَمَيْنِ

Habibi Muhammad, Muhammad,
Muhaaammad

حَبِيْبِيْ مُحَمَّدْ مُحَمَّدْ مُحَمَّدْ

Khayrul Mursaleen

خَيْرُ الْمُرْسَلِيْن

Your light is luminous, You are the owner of the souls, Many lovers went to the two holy
sanctuaries, My Beloved Prophet Muhammad (pbuh), the best of messengers

CHORUS

(Ya'Allah Ya Badi, Balighna Jamee') x2

(يَا الله يَا بَدِيْع، بَلِّغْنَا جَمِيْع) x٢

Hadra tash'shafee, Khayrul tha'qalayni

حَضْرَةَ الشَّفِيْع، خَيْرُ الثَّقَلَيْنِ

Habibi Muhammad, Muhammad,
Muhaaammad

حَبِيْبِيْ مُحَمَّدْ مُحَمَّدْ مُحَمَّدْ

Khayrul Mursaleen

خَيْرُ الْمُرْسَلِيْن

O Allah (AJ) the Incomparable Creator, grant us all the presence of the Intercessor, who
is the best of humans and jinn, My Beloved, Muhammad (pbuh), the Best of messengers

Ya Taybah

يَا طَيْبَة

Ya Taybah, Ya Taybah
Ya dawal 'ayana
Ishtaqna layk
(wal hawa nadaana) x2

يَا طَيْبَة، يَا طَيْبَة
يَا دَوَا الْعَيَانَا
إِشْتَقْنَالَك
(وَالْهَوَا نَادَانَا) ٢x

O Good One, O Good One, O the cure of my eyes
We are longing for you, And your love keeps calling us to be near you

Ya Ali, ibni Abi Talib
Minkumu, masdarul mawaahib
Hal tura, hal urali haajib
'indakum
(Afda'lul ghilmaana) x2

يَا عَلِيْ إِبْنِ أَبِيْ طَالِبْ
مِنْكُمُ مَصْدَرُالْمَوَاهِبْ
هَلْ تَرَا، هَلْ أَرَا لِي حَاجِبْ
عِنْدَكُمْ
(أَفْضَلُ الْغِلْمَانْ) ٢x

O Imam Ali, son of Abu Thalib, You are the door to the Prophet Muhammad (pbuh), who
is the source of Divine favors. We are seeing by your side the two great young men,
Imam Hassan (as) and Imam Hussain (as)

CHORUS

Asyadil Hassan wal Hussaini
Ilan Nabi qurrato 'aini
Ya shabaa bal janna'taini
Jaddukum
(saahibul Qur'ana) x2

أَسْيَادِيْ الْحَسَّنْ وَالْحُسَّيْنِ
إِلَي النَّبِيْ قَرَّةَ الْعَيْنِ
وَيَا شَبَابَ الْجَنَتَيْنِ
جَدُّكُمْ
(صَاحِبُ الْقُرْآنَ) ٢x

Our Masters, Imam Hassan (as) and Imam Hussain (as), They are the coolness of
Prophet's (pbuh) eyes. O the Youth of the Paradises, Your Grandfather (Prophet
Muhammad (pbuh)) is the owner of the holy Quran

CHORUS

اَللَّهُمَّ صَلِّ وَ سَلِّمْ وَ بَارِك عَلَيْهِ وَ عَلَي آلِهْ
Allahuma salli wa sallim wa barik 'alayhi wa 'ala alih
O Allah (AJ) send peace and blessings upon Prophet Muhammad (pbuh) and his family.

Ahmad Ya Habibi

اَحْمَدْ يَا حَبِيْبِيْ

أَحْمَدْ يَا حَبِيْبِيْ
أَحْمَدْ يَا حَبِيْبِيْ

**Ahmad ya Habibi
Ya Habibi, Salam 'Alayka,
Salam 'Alayka**

أَحْمَدْ يَا حَبِيْبِيْ
يَا حَبِيْبِيْ، سَلَّامْ عَلَيْكَ، سَلَّامْ عَلَيْكَ

**Ahmad ya Habibi,
Ahmad ya Habibi**

O my Beloved and my Master Prophet Ahmad (pbuh),
O my Beloved, Peace be upon you, Peace be upon you

يَاعَوْنَ الْغَرِيْب
يَا شَفِيْعَ الْخَلْقِ

**Ya noora zhalami
Ya Habibi, Salam 'Alayka,
Salam 'Alayka**

يَا نُوْرَ الظَّلَام
يَا حَبِيْبِيْ، سَلَّامْ عَلَيْكَ، سَلَّامْ عَلَيْكَ

**Ya awnal gharibi
Ya Shafi'al khalqi**

O the Supporter of the poor and helpless, O the light in the darkness,
O intercessor of the creation, O my Beloved, Peace be upon you

CHORUS

يَا أَبَا الْقَاسِم
يَا جَدَ الْحُسَّيْنِ

**Ya Abaz Zahrayee
Ya Habibi, Salam 'Alayka,
Salam 'Alayka**

يَا أَبَا الزَّهْرَاءِ
يَا حَبِيْبِيْ، سَلَّامْ عَلَيْكَ، سَلَّامْ عَلَيْكَ

**Ya abal Qaasemi
Ya Jaddal Hussaini**

O father of Qasim (as), O father of Zahra (as), O grandfather of Imam Hussain (as),
O my Beloved, Peace be upon you

CHORUS

يَا مُحْيِي الْقُلُوْب

يَا حَبِيْبِيْ ، سَلَّامْ عَلَيْكَ ، سَلَّامْ عَلَيْكَ

يَا طَهَ طَبِيْبِيْ

يَا قُرَّةَ العَيْنِ

Ya Taha Tabibi

Ya Qurratul `aini

Ya Muhyil qulubi

Ya Habibi, Salam 'Alayka,

Salam 'Alayka

O my healer Taha (Purified Guide), O reviver of hearts, O coolness to our eyes,
O my Beloved, Peace be upon you

CHORUS

يَا رَسُوْلَ اللهِ

يَا حَبِيْبِيْ ، سَلَّامْ عَلَيْكَ ، سَلَّامْ عَلَيْكَ

يَا صُفْوَةَ اللهِ

يَا حَبِيْبِ اللهِ

Ya Sufwat Allahi

Ya Habib Allahi

Ya Rasul Allahi

Ya Habibi, Salam 'Alayka,

Salam 'Alayka

O Allah's (AJ) elite, O Messenger of Allah (AJ), O Beloved of Allah (AJ),
O my Beloved, Peace be upon you!

CHORUS

اَللّٰهُمَّ صَلِّ وَ سَلِّمْ وَ بَارِكْ عَلَيْهِ وَ عَلَى آلِهْ

Allahuma salli wa sallim wa barik 'alayhi wa 'ala alih

O Allah (AJ) send peace and blessings upon Prophet Muhammad (pbuh) and his family.

Ya Zahra
يَا زَهْرَاءُ

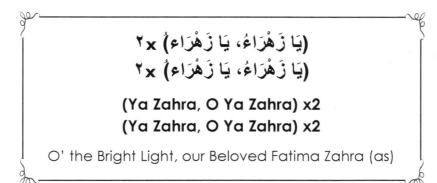

(يَا زَهْرَاءُ، يَا زَهْرَاءُ) x٢

(يَا زَهْرَاءُ، يَا زَهْرَاءُ) x٢

(Ya Zahra, O Ya Zahra) x2
(Ya Zahra, O Ya Zahra) x2

O' the Bright Light, our Beloved Fatima Zahra (as)

(زَهْرَاءُ نُوْرُ الْعَيْنِيْ

(هَكَذَا قَالَ الرَّسُوْلْ) x٢

Man azaha, yu'zini) x2
Fatima antel Batul

مَنْ آذَاهَا يُوْذِيْنِيْ) x٢

فَاطِمَةَ أَنْتِ الْبَتُوْلْ

(Zahra o Noorul 'ayni
(Hakaza qalar Rasul) x2

'Fatima Zahra is the light of my eyes, whoever caused her harm has caused me harm.' That is what the Prophet Muhammad (pbuh) was saying about his daughter. Our beloved Fatima, you are the Purified Light of Holy Quran

CHORUS

(فَاطِمَةَ لَكَ حُبِّيْ

(يَنْمُوْ دَوْمَا فِيْ قَلْبِيْ) x٢

Wa laki khoto darbi) x2
Hubbu Fatimal Batul

وَلَكِ خُطُوْ دَرْبِيْ) x٢

حُبُّ فَاطِمَةَ الْبَتُوْلْ

(Fatima laki hubbi
(Yanmu dauma fi Qalbi) x2

O Beloved Fatima, my love is for you, and my yearning is to be with you, Your love is forever in my heart and it continues to grow, the love of beloved Fatima, the Purified Light of Holy Quran

CHORUS

مَا بَقِيْتُ مِنْ دُهْرِيْ (x٢   (إِلَهِيْ زِدْ فِيْ عُمْرِيْ

حُبُّ فَاطِمَةَ الْبَتُوْلْ   (حُبٌّ فِيْ قَلْبِيْ يَجَرِيْ) x٢

(Illahi zid fi umri   **Ma baqitu min duhri) x2**

Hubbun fi Qalbi yajari x2   **Hubbu Fatimal Batul**

O Almighty God, please extend my life and for the remaining of my life, let this love continuously flow in my heart, the love of beloved Fatima, Purified Light of Holy Quran

CHORUS

بِمَوْلِدْ أَمُّ الْحَسَنَيْن (x٢   (صَلُوْ عَلَي طَهَ الزَّين

فَاطِمَة أَنْتِ الْبَتُوْلْ   (نُوْرُ سَاطِعٌ مُبِيْنْ) x٢

(Sallu 'Alaa Tahaz Zain   **Bi mawlid Ummil Hasanayn) x2**

Noorun sati'un Mubeen x2   **Fatima antel Batul**

Praise be upon Taha (the Purified and perfected Guide Sayyidina Muhammad (pbuh)), for the gift he gave us with the birth of Fatima, the mother of Imam Hassan (as) and Imam Hussain (as), a sparkling heavenly light. Our beloved Fatima, you are the Purified Light of Holy Quran

CHORUS

اَللَّهُمَّ صَلِّ وَ سَلِّمْ وَ بَارِكْ عَلَيْهِ وَ عَلَي اَلِهْ

Allahuma salli wa sallim wa barik 'alayhi wa 'ala alih

O Allah (AJ) send peace and blessings upon Prophet Muhammad (pbuh) and his family.

Habaha Rabbuha
حَبَاهَا رَبُّهَا

وَذِكْرًا فِيْ ذَرَا التَّقْوَى عَلِيًّا) x۲
حَبَاهَا اللهُ مَوْلُوْدًا زَكِيًّا

(حَبَاهَا رَبُّهَا قَلْبًا نَقِيًّا
وَنَالَتْ مَــرْيَمُ الْأَفْضَالَ لَمَّا

(Habaha Rabbuha, qalban naqiya
Wa naalat, Mariammul afdala lama

Wa zikran, fi zura taqwa 'aliya) x2
Habaa hAllahu mawludan zakiya

Her Lord gifted her with a pure heart and soul. Her reality is of an extreme piety, a high station of certainty, and nearness to her lord. The holy Maryam (Mary) was honoured and "chosen above all women of the world" by Allah (AJ) (Quran 3:42), to be gifted from her lord with a birth of a pure soul, without being touched by any mortal.

سَرَاى فِي الْمَسْجِدِ الْأَقْصَى، شَجِيًّا
مِنَّ الْمِحْرَابِ، تَرْفَعُهُ نَدِيَّا

حَمَامُ الْقُدْسِ مُشْتَاقٌ، لِصَوْتٍ
يُنَـاجِي اللهَ، فِيْ جَوْفِ الْلَّيَالِيْ

Hamamul Qudsi mushtaqun, li sawtin
Yunajillaha, fi jawfil layali

Sara fil Masjidil Aqsa, shajiya
Minal mihrabi tarfa 'uhu nadiya

The pigeons of the Al Quds (in Israel) were longing to hear the soft voice, that once floated sorrowfully and tenderly raised from the prayer chamber of the Al Aqsa Masjid; Pleading to Allah (AJ) in the depths of the nights.

تُسَاقِطْ فَوْقَهَا رُطَبًا جَنِيًّا
(وَحَنَّ الْمَاءُ، كَيْ يَجْرِيْ سَرِيًّا) ۲x

وَتَاقَتْ نَخْلَةَ الْمِيْلَادِ كَيْمَا
فَبَاتَ الْجِذْعُ، فِيْ شَوْقٍ إِلَيْهَا

Wa taqat nakhlatul miladi kayma
Fabatal jez'o, fi shawqin ilayha

Tusaqit fawqaha ruttaban Janiya
(Wa hannal Maa O, kay yajri sariya) x2

The blessed Mary with her immense certainty brought the palm tree to her presence, and merely commanded it to give its gifts. The palm tree was delighted to be of service to her and present her with its ripe dates. And the water also yearned to flow beneath her holy feet.

CHORUS

مِنَ الْوِجْدَانِ أَرْسِلْهُ ذَكِيًّا   سَلَامْ، يَا نَبِيَّ اللهِ عِيسَى

وَأَنْتَ الْغَيْثُ، جَسَّدَهُ نَبِيًّا   فَأَنْتَ الرُّوحُ، مِنْ رَبِّ الْبَرَايَا

Salam, ya NabiAllahi 'Isa   **Minal wijdani, ursilluhu zaykiya**

Fa antar Ruho, min rabbil baraya   **Wa antal ghaythu, jassada hu Nabiya**

Peace be upon you, O Prophet of Allah (AJ), Isa (Jesus) (pbuh), from the depth of the soul that purifies. May Allah (AJ) send peace and blessings upon you, and continuously dress you with His light and blessings. You are the holy spirit from the Lord, and you are a manifestation of the Lord's mercy in the form of a prophet.

نَقَطَ الْحَقَّ فِيْ مَهْدِ صَبِيًّا   جُعِلْتَ مُبَارَكًا، فِيْ كُلِّ حِينٍ

(رُفِعَتَّ، إِلَى جِنَانِ الْخُلْدِ حَيًّا) ٢x   وَمَا قَتَّلُوْكَ أَوْصَلَبُوْكَ، لَكِنْ

Ju'ilta mubarakan, fi kulli henin   **Naqat tan Haqqa, fi mahdin sabiya**

Wa maa qattaluka aw sabuluka, laken   **(Rufi'atta, ila jinanil khuldi Hayya) x2**

You are spreading Allah's (AJ) mercy and blessings at all time, wherever you go on this earth. You spoke the truth as an infant in your cradle. They did not kill you or crucify you, but you were raised to heavens to be eternally alive.

CHORUS

اَللّٰهُمَّ صَلِّ وَ سَلِّمْ وَ بَارِكْ عَلَيْهِ وَ عَلَى آلِه

Allahuma salli wa sallim wa barik 'alayhi wa 'ala alih

O Allah (AJ) send peace and blessings upon Prophet Muhammad (pbuh) and his family.

Ya Shafi' Al Wara

يَا شَفِيْعَ الْوَرَى

يَا نَبِيَّ الْهُدَى، سَلَامٌ عَلَيك

سَيِّدُ الْأَصْفِيَاء، سَلَامٌ عَلَيك

يَا شَفِيْعَ الْوَرَى، سَلَامٌ عَلَيك

خَاتِمُ الْأَنْبِيَاء، سَلَامٌ عَلَيك

Ya Shafi' Al Wara, Salamun 'Alayk
Khatimul Anbiya, Salamun 'Alayk

Ya Nabiy al Huda, Salamun 'Alayk
Sayyidul AsfiYa, Salamun 'Alayk

O Intercessor of mankind, peace be upon you; O Prophet of guidance, peace be upon you; The Seal of the prophets, peace be upon you; Master of the purified ones, peace be upon you

مَرْحَبًا مَرْحَبًا، سَلَامٌ عَلَيك

يَا حَبِيْبَ الْعُلَى، سَلَامٌ عَلَيك

أَحْمَدُ لَيْسَ مِثْلُكَ أَحَدٌ

وَاجِبٌ حُبُّكَ، عَلَى الْمَخْلُوقْ

Ahmadu' Layssa Mithluka ahadun
Wajibun Hubbuka Alal Makhlouq

Marhaban Marhaba, Salamun 'Alayk
Ya Habibal 'Ulaa, Salamun 'Alayk

O Ahmad (Prophet Muhammad (pbuh)), no one is like you, Greetings, peace be upon you, Your love is an obligation on the creation, O Beloved of the Sublime, peace be upon you

CHORUS

أَفْضَلُ الْأَنْبِيَاء، سَلَامٌ عَلَيك

صَاحِبَ الْإِهْتِدَاء، سَلَامٌ عَلَيك

أَعْظَمُ الْخَلْقِ، أَشْرَفُ الشُّرَفَاء

مَهْبِطُ الْوَحْيِ مَنْزَلِ الْقُرَانْ

A'zamul Khalqi, Ashrafu shurafaa
Mahbetul Wahyi Manzalil Quran

Afdhalul Anbiya, Salamun 'Alayk
Sahibal Ih'tida, Salamun 'Alayk

You are the Greatest and above all creation, the most Honourable, and the best of prophets, You are the base of revelation, the home of Quran, and the owner of guidance, peace be upon you

CHORUS

اِشْفَعْ لِي يَا حَبِيبِي يَوْمَ الْجَزَاء   أَنْتَ شَفِيعُنَا، سَلَامٌ عَلِيك

كُشِفَتْ مِنْكَ ظُلْمَةُ الظُّلَمَاء   أَنْتَ بَدْرُ الدُّجَى، سَلَامٌ عَلِيك

Ishfa' Li Ya Habibi Yawmal Jazaa   **Anta Shafi'una, Salamun Alayk**

Kushifat Minka Zulmatul Zulama'   **Anta Badrud Dujaa, Salamun 'Alayk**

Intercede for me O my Beloved, on the day of judgement. You are our Intercessor, you remove the oppressions and the oppressors (from the world), You are the perfect full moon on a dark night, peace be upon you

CHORUS

طَلَعَتْ مِنْكَ كَوْكَبُ الْعِرْفَانْ   أَنْتَ شَمْسُ الضُّحَى، سَلَامٌ عَلِيك

لَيْلَةَ الإِسْرَاء قَالَتِ الْأَنْبِيَاء   مَرْحَبًا مَرْحَبًا، سَلَامٌ عَلِيك

Tala 'at Minka Kawkabul Irfan   **Anta Shamsud Dhuha, Salamun 'Alayk**

Laylatul Isra qaalatil Anbiya   **Marhaban Marhaba, Salamun 'Alayk**

You are the sun of all knowers and the source of Divine realities. You emanate like the bright morning sun, peace be upon you, In the Night of your Ascension, all the prophets greeted you and said peace be upon you

CHORUS

مَقْصُدِي يَا حَبِيبِي لَيْسَّ سِوَاك   أَنْتَ مَقْصُودُنَا، سَلَامٌ عَلِيك

إِنَّكَ مَقْصَدِئ وَ مَلْجَئِي   إِنَّكَ مُدَّعَى، سَلَامٌ عَلِيك

Maqsudi Ya Habibi Layssa Siwak   **Anta Maqsuduna, Salamun 'Alayk**

Innaka Maqsadi Wa Maljaa'yee   **Innaka Mudda'a, Salamun 'Alayk**

My only aim is to reach your proximity O my Beloved, peace be upon you, You are my haven and my destination and my ultimate goal

CHORUS

أَفْضَلُ الْأَنْبِيَاء، سَلَامٌ عَلِيك   صَلَوَاتُ اللهِ، عَلَى الْمُصْطَفَى

مِنْهُمْ يَا مُصْطَفَى، سَلَامٌ عَلِيك   هَذَا أَوَّلُ غُلَامِكَ يَا سَيِّدِئ

Salawatullahe 'Alal Mustafa   **Afdhalul Anbiya, Salamun 'Alayk**

Hadha Awwalu Ghulamek Ya Sayyidi   **Minhum Ya Mustafa, Salamun 'Alayk**

May peace and blessings of Allah (AJ) be upon the Chosen One, the Best of all prophets, peace be upon you May you accept me as one of your servants, O my Master O Chosen One, peace be upon you

CHORUS

Ya Arhamar Rahimin
يَا أَرْحَمَ الرَّاحِمِينْ

يَا أَرْحَمَ الرَّاحِمِينْ، يَا أَرْحَمَ الرَّاحِمِينْ
يَا أَرْحَمَ الرَّاحِمِينْ، فَـرِّجْ عَلَى الْمُسْلِمِينْ

Ya Arhamar Rahimin, Ya Arhamar Rahimin
Ya Arhamar Rahimin, Farrij 'alal Muslimin

O Most Merciful of the merciful ones, Send an opening and salvation to all those who submit

يَا رَبَّنَا يَا كَرِيم
أَنْتَ الْجَوَادُ الْحَلِيم

يَا رَبَّنَا يَا رَحِيـم
وَأَنْتَ نِعْمَ الْمُعِين

Ya Rabbana Ya Karim
Antal Jawadul Haleem

Ya Rabbana Ya Rahim
Wa anta ni'mal Mu'yeen

O our Lord, the most Generous, the most Merciful! You are the One who gives freely, and You are the One with Forbearance, And the best One who supports

CHORUS

وَمَالَنَا رَبَّنَـا
يَاذَا الْعُلَا وَالْغِنَـا

سِـوَاكَ يَا حَسْبَنَـا
وَيَا قَـوِيٌ يَا مَتِين

Wa ma lana Rabbana
Ya dhal 'ula wal ghina

Sewaka ya Hasbana
Wa ya Qawi ya Mateen

Our Lord we have no one to rely on, except You are O Sufficient for us,
O Most High and Rich and owner of all treasures. O the most Strong and the Firm One!

CHORUS

وَلَيْسَ نَرْجُو سِوَاك
قَبْلَ الْفَنَا وَالْهَـلَاكْ

فَادْرِكْ إِلَـهِيْ دَرَاكْ
يَعُمُّ دُنْيَـا وَدِيـن

Wa laysa narju siwak
Qablal fana wal halak

Fadrik ilahi darak
Ya 'ummud duya wa din

O my Lord, we seek none but You, watch over us, support us and protect our faith before the world comes to an end

CHORUS

بِجَاهِ طَهَ الرَّسُولْ   جُدْ رَبَّنَا بِالْقَـبُولْ
وَهَبْ لَنَا كُلَّ سُـؤَلْ   رَبِّي اسْتَجِبْ لِي، أَمِـين

Bi jahi Taha Rasul   **Jud rabbana bil qabul**
Wa hab lana kulla sol   **Rabbis tajib li Ameen**

For the sake of Taha (the Purified Guide), the Messenger, O our Lord, accept us as Your servants. Please grant us your favors and accept our prayers – Ameen!

CHORUS

وَاسْتُرْلِي كُلّ الْعُيُوبْ   وَاغْفِرْلِي كُلّ الذُّنُوبْ
وَاكْفِ أَذَى الْمُؤْذِين   وَاكْشِفْ لِي كُلّ الْكُرُوبْ

Waghfir li kullidh dhunub   **Wastur li kulli 'uyub**
Wakshif li kullil kurub   **Wa kfi'adha mu-dhin**

And forgive me all my sins, and cover all my flaws and shortcomings,
And lift from me all difficulties, and save me from the harm of those who want to hurt me

CHORUS

إِذَا دَنَا الْإِنْصِـرَامْ   وَاخْتِمْ بِأَحْسَنْ خِتَامْ
وَزَادَ رَشْـحُ الْجَبِين   وَحَانَ حِيْنُ الْحِمَامْ

Wakhtim bi ahsan khitam   **Idha danal inSiram**
Wa hana hinul himam   **Wa zada rashhul jab'een**

And let my life end with goodness and in best of Iman (faith), when death approaches,
And when the time for trials arrive, and the sweat of the brow increases

CHORUS

عَلَى شَفِـيْعُ الْإِنَـامْ   ثَمَ الصَّلَاةُ وَالسَّلَامْ
والصَّحْبِ وَالتَّابِعِين   وَالْآلَ نِعْمَ الْكِرَامْ

Thummas salat was salam   **'Ala shafiul inam**
Wal aali ni'mal kiram   **Was-sahbi wat-tabi'een**

Then praise and send blessings, upon the Intercessor of all nations and upon his most honored family, and his holy companions, and those who follow him in deeds and actions

CHORUS

Rabbi Faghfir li Dhunubi

رَبِّي فَأغْفِرْلِيْ ذِنُوْبِي

بِبَرْكَةِ الْهَادِيْ مُحَمَّدْ ، يَا الله | (رَبِّي فَأغْفِرْلِيْ ذِنُوْبِيْ، يَا الله)x٢

**(Rabbi faghfir li dhunubi Ya Allah
Bi barkatil Hadi Muhammad Ya Allah) x2**

O my Lord, forgive my sins, O Allah (AJ),
By the blessings of the Perfected guide, Prophet Muhammad (pbuh), O Allah (AJ)

فِيْ جِوَارِه خَيْرَ مَقْعَدْ، يَا الله | رَبِّي بَلِّغْنَا بِجَاهِهْ، يَا الله

**Rabbi balighna bi jahi, ya Allah
Fi jiwari khayra maq'ad, ya Allah**

O my Lord, let us reach (our destination), for the sake of Prophet Muhammad's (pbuh)
high station (with You), In his proximity is the best place to stay

CHORUS

أَشْرَفَ الرُّسْلِ مُحَمَّدْ، يَا الله | وَصَلَاةُ اللهِ تَغْشَى، يَا الله

**Wa salatullahi taghsha, Ya Allah
Ashrafar Rusli Muhammad, Ya Allah**

May Allah's (AJ) blessings shower him, Prophet Muhammad (pbuh) is the noblest of the
Messengers

CHORUS

كُلَّ حِيْنٍ يَا تَجَدَّدْ، يَا الله | وَسَلَامٌ مُسْتَمِرٌّ، يَا الله

**Wa salamun mustamirrun, Ya Allah
Kulla hinin ya tajaddad, Ya Allah**

Peace be upon him, Prophet Muhammad (pbuh), Continuously and renewed at every
moment

CHORUS

يَا رَسُوْلُ اللهِ أَهْلاً، يَا الله   بِكَ إِنَا بِكَ نُسْعَدْ، يَا الله

Ya Rasulullahi ahlan, Ya Allah
Bika inna bika nus'ad, Ya Allah

Welcome O Messenger of Allah (AJ) Welcome, For verily with you is our joy and happiness

CHORUS

وَ بِجَاهِهْ يَا إِلَهِيْ، يَا الله   جُدْ وَ بَلِّغْ كُلَّ مَقْصَدْ، يَا الله

Wa bijahi, ya ilahi, Ya Allah
Jud wa balligh kulla maqsad, Ya Allah

And by Prophet Muhammad's (pbuh) high honored station, O our Lord,
Give us generously and grant us all that we are in need of

CHORUS

وَاهْدِنَا نَهْجَ سَبِيْلِهْ، يَا الله   كَيْ بِهِ نُسْعَدْ وَنُرْشَدْ، يَا الله

Wahdina nahja sabilih, Ya Allah
Kay bihi nus'ad wa nurshad, Ya Allah

Guide us with his methods and directions, O Allah (AJ),
So that we receive happiness and guidance, O Allah (AJ)

CHORUS

اَللّٰهُمَّ صَلِّ وَ سَلِّمْ وَ بَارِكْ عَلَيْهِ وَ عَلَي آلِهْ

Allahuma salli wa sallim wa barik 'alayhi wa 'ala alih

O Allah (AJ) send peace and blessings upon Prophet Muhammad (pbuh) and his family.

Ya Hanana

يَاهَنَانَا

(Zahara ad-dinul mu'ayyad

Bi zuhurin Nabi Ahmad) x2

Ya Hannana bi Muhammad

Dhalikal fadhlu min Allahhhh

ALLAH!

(Ya Hannana, Ya Hannana) x4

ظَهَرَ الدِّيْنُ الْمُؤَيَّدْ

بِظُهُوْرِ النَّبِيْ اَحْمَدْx٢

يَاهَنَّانَا بِمُحَمَّدْ

ذَلِكَ الْفَضْلُ مِنَ اللهِ....

اَللهُ!

يَاهَنَّانَا، يَاهَنَّانَا x٤

Allah's (AJ) eternal religion manifested by arrival and birth of the Perfected Guide, Prophet Ahmad (pbuh). Our peace and joy can only be achieved by the presence of Muhammad (pbuh) whom is the grace and bounty of Allah (AJ)

Khus'sa bis sab 'il mathani

Wa hawa lutfal ma'ani

Malahu fil khalqi thani

Wa 'alayhi anzal Allahhhh...ALLAH!

(Ya Hannana, Ya Hannana) x4

خُصَّ بِالسَّبْعِ الْمَثَانِيْ

وَحَوَا لُطْفَ الْمَعَانِيْ

مَا لَهُ فِي الْخَلْقِ ثَانِيْ

وَعَلَيْهِ اَنْزَلْ اللهُ... اللهُ!

يَاهَنَّانَا، يَاهَنَّانَا x٤

He was solely gifted with the seven holy verses of Surat Al Fatiha, And he encompassed the finest qualities, There is nobody in creation like him, And Allah (AJ) has bestowed upon him (holy Quran), O our joy, O our joy

CHORUS

Min Makatin, lama zahar

Li ajlihin shaqal qamar

Waf'takharat aalo mudhar

Bihi 'ala kullil anammmi...ALLAH!

(Ya Hannana, Ya Hannana) x4

مِنْ مَكَّةٍ، لَمَّا ظَهَرْ

لِأَجْلِهِ انْشَقَّ الْقَمَرْ

وَافْتَخَرَتْ اَلْ مُضَرْ

بِهِ عَلَى كُلِّ الْآنَامِ... اَللهُ!

يَاهَنَّانَا، يَاهَنَّانَا x٤

When he appeared from Makkah, He split the moon with a sign of his finger, And he was the pride of Al-Mudar's family, He is above all mankind, O our joy.

CHORUS

Salu 'ala khairul anami

صَلّوا عَلَى خَيرِ الْأَنَام

Al Mustafa badrit ta'maami

اَلْمُصْطَفَى بَدْرِالتَّمَام

Salu 'alayhi wa salimu

صَلّوا عَلَيْهِ وَسَلِّمُوا

Yashfa' lana yawma zihammi...ALLAH!

يَشْفَعْ لَنَا يَوْمَ الزِّحَام ... اَللهِ!

(Ya Hannana, Ya Hannana) x4

يَاهَنَّانَا، يَاهَنَّانَا x٤

Praise the best of creation, Al-Mustafa (pbuh) the full moon, Send peace and blessings upon him, Pray that he intercede for us on judgment day

CHORUS

اَللّهُمَّ صَلِّ وَ سَلِّمْ وَ بَارِكْ عَلَيْهِ وَ عَلَي اَلِهْ

Allahuma salli wa sallim wa barik 'alayhi wa 'ala alih

O Allah (AJ) send peace and blessings upon Prophet Muhammad (pbuh) and his family.

Part C

Hadra

(The Presence)

حَضْرَة

Ya Nabi Salam 'Alayka
يَا نَبِيْ سَلَامْ عَلَيْكَ

يَا نَبِيْ سَلَامْ عَلَيْكَ
يَا حَبِيبْ سَلَامْ عَلَيْكَ

يَا رَسُولْ سَلَامْ عَلَيْكَ
صَلَوَاتُ اللهِ عَلَيْكَ

Ya Nabi Salam 'Alayka
Ya Habib salam 'Alayka

Ya Rasul Salam 'Alayka
Salawatullah 'Alayka

O Prophet, peace be upon you, O Messenger, peace be upon you
O my Beloved, peace be upon you, Praises of Allah (AJ) be upon you

أَشْرَقَ الْكَوْنُ اِبْتِهَاجًا
وَ لِأَهْلِ الْكَوْنِ أَنْسٌ

بِوُجُودِ الْمُصْطَفَى أَحْمَدْ
وَ سُرُورٌ قَدْ تَجَدَّدْ

Ashraqal kawnu ibtihajan
Wa li ahlil kawni unsun

Bi wujudil Mustafa Ahmad
Wa sururun qad tajaddad

The sun of realities rose and lit up the world and the creation rejoiced, With the birth of
the Chosen One Ahmad (pbuh), Everyone in the universe was joyful, And happy with
this renewal and glad tidings from God

CHORUS

فَهَزَارُ الْيُمْنِ غَرَدْ
فَاقَ فِي الْحُسْنِ تَفَرَّدْ

فَاطْرَبُوْا يَا أَهْلَ الْمَثَانِيْ
وَاسْتَضِيْوُا بِجَمَالٍ

Fatrabu ya ahlal mathani
Wastadio bi Jamalin

Fa hazarul yumni gharrad
Faqa fil Husni tafarrad

The nightingale is singing: 'Be delighted and grateful, O people of the heavens and
earth with this good fortune. And ask for guidance from his magnificent character, and
seek Divinely light from his illuminous holy face

CHORUS

مُسْتَمِّرٍ لَيْسَ يَنْفَدْ
جَمَعَ الْفَخْرُ الْمُؤَبَّدْ

وَ لَنَا الْبُشْرَا بِسَعْدٍ
حَيْثُ أُوْتِيْنَا عَطَاءً

Wa lanal bushra bi sa'din
Haythu utina 'ata an

Mustamirrin laysa yanfad
Jama'l fakhrul muabbad

We received the good news, With continuous and never ending happiness, As we were
granted the greatest blessing of birth of Prophet Muhammad (pbuh) whom
encompasses eternal glory and honor for this life and hereafter

CHORUS

أَشْرَقَ الْبَدْرُ عَلَيْنَا
مِثْلَ حُسْنِكَ مَا رَأَيْنَا

فَاخْتَفَتْ مِنْهُ الْبُدُورِ
قَطُّ يَا وَجْهَ السُّرُورِ

Ashraqal Badru 'Alaina
Misla Husnik ma ra-ayna

Fakhtafat Minhul Buduro
Qattu ya Wajhas Surori

Your full moon rises over us, the other moon disappears, We never saw like your beauty and perfection, O holy Face of Divine happiness

CHORUS

أَنْتَ شَمْسٌ أَنْتَ بَدْرٌ
أَنْتَ إِكْسِيْرُ وَغَالِي

أَنْتَ نُورٌ فَوْقَ نُورٍ
أَنْتَ مِصْبَاحُ الصُّدُورِ

Anta Shamsun anta Badrun
Anta Iksiru Wa ghali

Anta Noorun fawqa Noori
Anta Misbahus Suduri

You are the Sun of universes, You are the perfect Moon, You are the light upon lights, You are the true alchemist that prufies and illuminates our souls, You are the divinely light in our hearts

CHORUS

يَا حَبِيبِي يَا مُحَمَّدْ
يَا مُؤَيَّدْ يَا مُمَجَّدْ

يَا عَرُوسَ الْخَافِقين
يَا إِمَامَ الْقَبْلَتَيْنِ

Ya Habibi ya Muhammad
Ya muayyad ya Mumajjad

Ya Arosal Khafiqayni
Ya Imamal Qiblatayni

O my beloved, O Muhammad (saws), O star of the East and the West, O supporter, O`praised one, O Imam and leader of both Qiblas (prayer direction)

CHORUS

فَلِرَبِّيْ كُلُّ حَمْدٍ
إِذْ حَبَانَا بِوُجُودِ

جَلَّ أَنْ يَحْصُرَهُ الْعَدْ
مُصْطَفَي الْهَادِيْ مُحَمَّدْ

Fa li rabbi kullu hamdin
Idh Habana bi wujudi

Jalla an yahsuru hul'ad
Mustafal Hadi Muhammad

All praises to my Lord and our countless gratitude, For bestowing upon us the presence and birth of His Beloved Muhammad (pbuh), the Chosen one, the most Perfected Guide. We are eternally grateful.

CHORUS

Ya Imamar Rusli

يَا إِمَامَ الرُّسْلِ

أَنْتَ بَابُ اللهِ مُعْتَمَدِيْ	يَا إِمَامَ الرُّسْلِ يَا سَنَدِيْ
يَا رَسُوْلَ اللهِ خُذْ بِيَدِيْ	فَبِدُنْيَايَ وَ آخِرَتِيْ

Ya imamar Rusli ya sanadi	**Anta babullahi mu'tamadi**
Fabi dunyaya wa akhirate	**Ya RasulAllahi khudh biyadi**

O Leader of the messengers, You are the door to Allah (AJ), You are the advocate in Divine Presence. I rely on your intercession. Please take my hand (bayah) and save me from harm and difficulties here and hereafter, O Messenger of Allah (Prophet Muhammad (pbuh))

مَا الْمُعَافَى وَالسَّقِيْمُ سَوَى	قَسَمًا بِالنَّجْمِ حِيْنَ هَوَى
حُبُّ مَوْلَى الْعُرْبِ وَالْعَجَمِ	فَاخْلَعِ الْكَوْنَيْنِ عَنْكَ سِوَى

Qasaman bin najmi hina hawa	**Mal mu'afa waSsaqimu sawa**
Fakhla'il kawnayni 'anka siwa	**Hubbu mawlal 'urbi wal 'ajami**

I swear "by the star in descent" (Quran, 53:1), Being healthy and sick are not alike, So I renounce both worlds, For the Love of the Master of the Arabs and Non-Arabs (Prophet Muhammad (pbuh))

CHORUS

غَوْثُ أَهْلِ الْبَدْوِ وَالْحَضَرِ	سَيِّدُ السَّادَاتِ مِنْ مُضَرِ
مَنْبَعُ الْأَحْكَامِ وَالْحِكَمِ	صَاحِبُ الْآيَاتِ وَالسُّوَرِ

Sayyidus sadati min mudari	**Ghawthu ahlil badwi wal hadari**
Sahibul aayati wassuwari	**Manba'ul ahkami wal hikami**

O Master of the masters of people of Mudar, You are the Saviour of people of the desert and the cities, You are the Owner of the verses and chapters of holy Quran, and the Source of laws, regulations and wisdom

CHORUS

وَسَجَايَاهُ وَسِيْرَتُـهُ
عَدْلُ أَهْلِ الْحِلِّ وَالْحِرَم

قَمَرٌ طَابَتْ سَرِيْرَتُـهُ
صَفْوَةُ الْبَـارِيْ وَخِيْرَتُهُ

Qamarun Tabat sariratuHu
Safwtul bari wa khiratuHu

Wa sajayaHu wa siratuHu
'Adlu ahlil hilli wal harami

Like a moon, he is good and wholesome in his intention, his character & his way of life,
He is the purest elect/ultimate choice of the Creator. He is the most trustworthy/a
righteous witness for people of upright and wrongdoing

CHORUS

مِثْلَ طَهَ فِي الْوَرَا بَشَرَا
طَاهِرُ الْأَخْلَاقِ وَالشِّيَمِ

مَا رَأَتْ عَيْنٌ وَلَيْسَ تَرَا
خَيْرُ مَنْ فَوْقَ الثَّرَاءَ سَرَا

Mara at 'aynun wa laysa tara
Khayru man fawqa thara asara

Mithla Taha fil wara bashara
Tahirul akhlaqe wa shiyami

No eyes has seen or will ever see, A human being like the Purified Guide, Taha (Prophet
Muhammad (pbuh)), He is the best of whomever left traces on earth, He is the purest
in manners and noble in his character

CHORUS

اَلَّلهُمَّ صَلِّ وَ سَلِّمْ وَ بَارِكْ عَلَيْهِ وَ عَلَي آلِهْ
Allahuma salli wa sallim wa barik 'alayhi wa 'ala alih
O Allah (AJ) send peace and blessings upon Prophet Muhammad (pbuh) and his family.

Burdah Sharif

بُرْدَه شَرِيف

الله الله الله

الله الله الله

الله يا مَوْلَانَا

رَبِّي أَنْظُرْ حَالِي

Allah Allah Allah
Allah Allah Allah

Allah Ya Mawlana
Rabbi Unzur halee

Allah (AJ), O Our Master, O My Lord gaze upon me and my condition

مَوْلَا يَا صَلِّي وَسَلِّمْ دَائِماً أَبَدَا   عَلَى حَبِيْبِكَ خَيْرِ الْخَلْقِ كُلِّهِمِ

Mawla Ya Salli Wa Sallim Da'iman 'Abadan
'Ala Habibika Khayril Khalqi kulli himin

O` my Lord, send peace and blessings continously, repeatedly, and eternally
Upon Your Beloved Muhammad (pbuh), who is the best of all creation

CHORUS

يَارَبِّي بِالْمُصْطَفَى بَلِّغْ مَقَاصِدَنَا   وَاغْفِرْ لَنَا مَا مَضَى يَا وَاسِعَ الْكَرَمِ

Ya rabbi bil Mustafa, baligh maqasidana
Waghfir lana maa madha ya wasi`al karami

O my Lord, By means of the Chosen One (Muhammad (pbuh)),
Forgive us our past sins, O All Comprehending, and the most Generous

CHORUS

مُحَمَّدٌ سَيِّدُ الْكَوْنَيْنِ وَالثَّقَلَيْنِ   خَيْرُ الْفَرِيقَيْنِ مِنْ عُرْبٍ وَمِنْ عَجَمِ

Muhammadun sayyidul kawnayni wa thaqalayn
Khayrul fariqayni min 'urbin wa min 'ajami

Prophet Muhammad (pbuh) is the Master of the Two Worlds, and master of the Human
and Jinn. He is the best of all Arabs and non-Arabs.

CHORUS

فَـاقَ الـنَّبِيِّينَ فِيْ خَلْقٍ وَفِيْ خُلُقٍ   وَلَـمْ يُدَانُـوْهُ فِيْ عِلْمٍ وَلَا كَرَمِ

Faqan Nabiyyina fi khalqin wa fi khuluqin
Wa lam yudanuhu fi 'ilmin wa la karami

He surpasses all Prophets in his form and character
None of them can reach the level of his knowledge and generosity

CHORUS

وَكُلُّـهُمْ مِنْ رَسُوْلِ اللهِ مُلْتَمِسٌ   غَرْفاً مِنَ الْبَحْرِ أَوْ رَشْفاً مِنَ الدِّيَمِ

Wa kulluhum min Rasulillahi multamisun
Gharfan minal bahri aw rashfan minad diyami

All of them come and take from Allah's (AJ) Messenger, some take a handful of his
ocean or some sip of his continuous rains

CHORUS

هُوَ الْحَبِيبُ الّذِي تُرْجَى شَفَاعَتُهُ   لِكُلِّ هَوْلٍ مِنَ الْأَهْوَالِ مُقْتَحِمِ

Huwal Habibul ladhi turja shafa'atuhu
Li kulli hawlin minal ahwali muqtahami

He is the Beloved of Allah (AJ), whom we rely on and seek his intercession.

CHORUS

وَلَنْ يَضِيْقَ رَسُوْلَ اللهِ جَاهُكَ بِيْ   إِذَا الْكَرِيْمُ تَجَلَّى بِاسْمِ مُنْتَقِـمِ

Wa lan yadiqa RasulAllahi jahuka bi
Idhal karimu tajalla bismi muntaqimi

And O Messenger of Allah (AJ), your exalted status will not diminish, From your
intercession for me, when the Most Bountiful manifests with the Name of Avenger

CHORUS

فَإِنَّ مِنْ جُوْدِكَ الدَّنْيَا وَضَرَّتَهَا   وَمِنْ عُلُومِكَ عِلْمَ اللَّوْحِ وَالْقَلَمِ

Fa inna min judika dunya wa darrataha
Wa min 'ulumika 'ilmal Lawhi wal Qalami

For verily amongst the bounties that Allah (AJ) granted you is this world and all of the
heavens, And of your knowledge is knowledge of the Preserved Tablets and the Pen

CHORUS

يَا نَفْسُ لَا تَقْنَطِيْ مِنْ زَلَّةٍ عَظُمَتْ   إِنَّ الْكَبَائِرَ فِي الْغُفْرَانِ كَاللَّمَمِ

Ya nafsu la taqnati min zallatin 'azumat
Innal kabayera fil ghufrani kallamami

O my self do not despair due to your grave sins,
Truly even the greatest sins when they are pardoned are minor

CHORUS

لَعَلَّ رَحْمَةَ رَبِّيْ حِيْنَ يَقْسِـمُهَا   تَأْتِي عَلَى حَسَبِ الْعِصْيَانِ فِي الْقِسَمِ

L'alla rahmata Rabbi hina yaqsimuha
Tati 'ala hasabil 'isyani fil qisami

Perhaps when the mercy of my Lord is distributed, It would be distributed in accordance
to our sins

CHORUS

وَالْطُفْ بِعَبْدِكَ فِي الدَّارَيْنِ إِنَّ لَـهُ   صَبْراً مَتَى تَدْعُهُ الْأَهْوَالُ يَنْهَـزِمِ

Waltuf bi'abdika fiddarayni inna laHu
Sabran mata tad'uhul ahwalu yanhazimi

Please be kind to Your servant in both worlds, for verily, my patience runs out, When I am
tested and face hardships (calamities)

CHORUS

وَإِذَنْ لِسُحْبِ صَلَاةٍ مِنْكَ دَائِمَـةٍ   عَلَى النَّبِي بِمُنْهَلٍ وَمُنْسَجِمِ

Wa dhan lisuhbi Salatin minka daayematin
'AlanNabiyi bi munhalin wa munsajimi

And order clouds of blessings (salutations) from you continously, abundantly and gently,
Upon the Prophet (Muhammad (pbuh))

CHORUS

ثُمَّ الرِّضَا عَنْ أَبِي بَكْرٍ وَعَنْ عُمَرٍ   وَعَنْ عَلِيٍّ وَعَنْ عُثْمَانَ ذِي الْكَرَمِ

Thummar rida `an Abi bakrin wa `an `Umarin,
Wa `an `Aliyyin wa `an `Uthmana dhil karami

Then upon our masters Abu Bakr (as), `Umar (as), `Uthman (as), and Imam 'Ali (as), the
Perfected guides and deputies of Prophet (saws). Whom have achieved Allah's (AJ)
satisfaction.

CHORUS

وَالآلِ وَالصَّحْبِ ثَمَّ التَّابِعِينَ لَهُمْ   أَهْلُ التَّقَى وَالنّقَا وَالْحِلْمِ وَالْكَرَمِ

Wal aali wasSahbi thumma tabi'yena lahum
Ahlut tuqa wannuqa wal hilmi wal karami

And O Allah (AJ), send peace and blessings upon his holy family and his holy companions, then upon those who follow them in deed and action, Whom are the people of piety, knowledge, clemency, and generosity

CHORUS

Qul Ya 'Azeem

قُلْ يَا عَظِيمُ

قَدْ هَمَّنَا هَمٌّ عَظِيمْ
يَهُوْنُ بِإِسْمِكَ يَاعَظِيمْ

قُلْ يَا عَظِيمْ، أَنْتَ الْعَظِيمْ
وَكُلُّ هَمٍّ هَمَّنَا

Qul ya 'Azeem, antal 'Azeem
Wa kullu ham'mun hammana

Qad hammanaa hammun 'Azeem
Ya hunu bismika ya 'Azeem

Say O Magnificent! You are the Almighty One. We have been afflicted with a grave concern. And every concern we are worried about becomes easy, With the mentioning of Your Name, O the most Magnificent

أَنْتَ اللَّطِيفْ، لَطِيفٌ لَمْ تَزَلْ
مِنْ فَادِحِ الْخَطْبِ الشَّدِيد

أَنْتَ الْقَدِيمْ، قَدِيمٌ فِي الْأَزَلْ
عَنَّا أَزِلْ، مَا قَدْ نَزَل

Antal qadeem, qadeemun fil azal
'Anna azil, maa qad nazal

Antal lateef, lateefun lam tazal
Min fadihil, khatbish shaded

You are the ancient one, O preternal one, You are The Subtle, with everlasting subtleness, Remove from us what has befallen us of grave difficulties and afflictions

CHORUS

بَاقِي غَنِي، غَنِيٌّ مَاجِدُ (الله)
بَـــرٌّ رَؤُوْفْ، رَؤُوْفٌ بِالْعَبِيد

حَيٌّ قَدِيمْ، قَدِيمٌ وَاجِدُ (الله)
عَدْلُ إِلَـهْ، إِلَـهٌ وَاحِدُ

Hayyun Qadeem, Qadeemun Wajidu
(Allah!)
Adlun Ilah, Ilahun Wahidu

Baqi Ghani, ghaniyun Majidu
(Allah!)
Barrun Rauf, Raufun bil 'abeed

O Ever-living and preternal Lord, Possesser of everything (Allah (AJ)), the Ever-lasting, the Generous One, the Rich and Most Glorious (Allah (AJ)). The All-Just God, the One and Only God. The Beneficent God is the most Subtle. He is affectionate, kind and gentle with His servant

CHORUS

وَلِلنَّبِيْ صَلِّي يَا سَلاَمْ   مِنّا صَلاَةٍ، مَع سَلاَمْ

يَوْمَ الْجَزَاءِ، امْنَحْنَا سَّلاَمْ   مِمَّا نَخَافُ يَا مَجِيدْ

Wa linNabbi salli ya salaam   **Minna salaatun, ma'a salaam**
Yawmal jazaa, nahnas salaam   **Mimmaa nakhafu ya Majeed**

And upon the Prophet of Peace, send greetings and blessings from us. Grant us safety on Day of Judgment from all things which we fear of suffering and difficulties, O Glorious One

CHORUS

وَالْآَلِ وَالصَّحْبِ الْأَسُود   سَادُوا بِهِ بِيْضاً وَسُــــود

لَا سِيَمَا مَاحِي الْحَـسُود   سَيْفُ اللهِ، إبْنِ الْوَلِيــدْ

Wal aali wassahbil usood   **saadu bihi bedan wa sood**
laa siyama maahil hasood   **sayfu' ilaah, ibnil Waleed**

And send peace and blessings upon the lions from the Family and Companions of Prophet Muhammad (pbuh). They became leaders of the Nation through their love for Prophet (pbuh) regardless of being white or black, especially the one who wiped out great armies, the Sword of Allah (AJ), Khalid son of al-Waleed

CHORUS

اَللَّهُمَّ صَلِ وَ سَلِّمْ وَ بَارِكْ عَلَيْهِ وَ عَلَي اَلِهْ
Allahuma salli wa sallim wa barik 'alayhi wa 'ala alih
O Allah (AJ) send peace and blessings upon Prophet Muhammad (pbuh) and his family.

Ya Abaz Zahra (saw)

يَاأَبَا الزَّهْرَاء(ص)

(Ya Abaz Zahraa, Billadhi Sanak) x2

(يَاأَبَا الزَّهْرَاء، بِالَّذِيْ صَنَاكَ) x٢

La Tukhayyibna Ya Sayyidi, Nahnu Jiranak

لا تُخَيِّبْنَا يَاسِيدِي، نَحْنُ جِيرَانَكْ

Ya Sayyidi Nahnu Jiranak

يَاسِيدِي نَحْنُ جِيْرَانَكْ

Allahu Allah Allah, Allahu Rabbi

اللهُ الله الله، اللهُ رَبِّيْ

'Awnee wa Hasbi, Mali Siwa Hu

عَوْنِيْ وَحَسْبِيْ مَا لِيْ سِوَاهُوْ

O Father of Fatima Zahra (Prophet Muhammad (pbuh)), By the One Who Protects you,
Don't close your door and don't turn away from us,
Let us draw near to you, O my master let us draw near,
Allah (AJ) is my Lord, He is the One who helps me and He is
Sufficient for me, I have no one except Him (Hu)

(Rawhu wa Rayhan, Ma Baynal Khullan) x2

(رَوْحُ وَرَيْحَانْ، مَّا بَيْنَ الْخُلَّانْ) x٢

Jannatur Ridwan, Ya Sayyidi fi hadratina

جَنَّةَ الرِّضْوَانْ يَاسِيدِيْ فِيْ حَضْرَتِنَا

Ya Sayyidi fi hadratina, Allah Allah

يَاسِيدِيْ فِيْ حَضْرَتِنَا، الله الله

Rest and satisfaction among intimate friends, Your presence is the 'Garden of Delights'
of Paradise, O My master Muhammad (pbuh)

CHORUS

(Hadratul Qudos, mahya lin nufus) x2

(حَضْرَةُ الْقُدُّوسْ، مَحْيَا لِلنّفُوسْ) x٢

Jannatul Firdausa Ya Sayyidi, Tahtaju ilayna

جَنَّةَ الْفِرْدَوْسَ يَاسِيدِيْ، تَحْتَاجُ إِلَيْنَا

Ya Sayyidi Tahtaju ilayna Allah Allah

يَاسِيدِيْ تَحْتَاجُ إِلَيْنَا، الله الله

You are the Holy Presence and the reviver of the souls, the Ferdaws` Paradise (7th
Heaven) is in desperate need of your light and presence, O My Master Muhammad
(pbuh)

CHORUS

(Min Khamril 'Irfaan, suqyina Qinaan) x2

(مِنْ خَمْرِ الْعِرْفَانْ، سُقِيْنَا قَنَنْ) x٢

Mey Yadil wildana Ya Sayyidi Mukhalladina

مِنْ يَدِ الْوِلْدَانْ يَاسِيدِيْ، مُخَلَّدِيْنَ

Ya Sayyidi Mukhalladina, Allah Allah

يَاسِيدِيْ مُخَلَّدِيْنَ ، الله الله

The Gnostics in their ecstasy drink the nectar that "will be circulated among them a cup
from a clear-flowing fountain" (Quran 37:45) from the hands of the ever-living youth

CHORUS

(Haalul 'Aarifeen, Mutaqabeleen) x2
'Aala Sururi Ya Sayyidi Mustabshirina
Ya Sayyidi Mustabshirina, Allah Allah

(حَالُ أَلْعَارِفِيْنْ مُتَقَابِلِينْ) x٢
عَلَى سُرُرٍ يَاسِيدِيْ، مُسْتَبْشِرِيْنَ
يَاسِيدِي مُسْتَبْشِرِيْنَ، الله الله

"In Gardens of Heaven", the Gnostics "Facing each other upon Thrones of honour"
(Quran 37:43-44) in an ecstatic state and good spirits

CHORUS

(Abnahul Hadrah, lahumul Bushraa) x2
Min Qablil ukhraa Ya Sayyidi Mu'azzazina
Ya Sayyidi Mu'azzazina, Allah Allah

(أَبْنَاءُ الْحَضْرَة لَهُمُ الْبُشْرَى) x٢
مِنْ قَبْلِ الْأَخْرَى يَاسِيدِيْ، مُعَزَّزِيْنَ
يَاسِيدِي مُعَزَّزِيْنَ، الله الله

The Children of the Presence (family of Prophet Muhammad (pbuh)), for them is glad
tiding, They are honored above all mankind before the rest, O my Master they are
honoured

CHORUS

('Ibaadur Rahman,Fi Kulli Zamaan) x2
Lahumul Amaan Ya Sayyidi, Mutma innena
Ya Sayyidi Mutma innena, Allah Allah

(عِبَادُ الرَّحْمَانْ، فِي كُلِّ زَمَانْ) x٢
لَهَمُ الْأَمَانْ يَاسِيدِيْ، مُطْمَئِنِينَ
يَاسِيدِي مُطْمَئِنِينَ، الله الله

The Servants of the Most Compassionate, at all time have safety and certainty, O my
Master, they have certainty

CHORUS

اَللّٰهُمَّ صَلِّ وَ سَلِّمْ وَ بَارِكْ عَلَيْهِ وَ عَلَي آلِهْ
Allahuma salli wa sallim wa barik 'alayhi wa 'ala alih
O Allah (AJ) send peace and blessings upon Prophet Muhammad (pbuh) and his family.

Ya Muhammad
يَا مُحَمَّد

(يَا مُحَمَّدْ يَا مُحَمَّدْ، يَا مُحَمَّدْ) x٢   (صَلَوَاتُ الله عَلَيْكَ سَيِّدْ مُحَمَّدْ) x٢

(Ya Muhammad, Ya Muhammad, YA MUHAMMAD) x2
(Salawatullah 'Alayka Sayyid Muhammad) x2

O our Master Prophet Muhammad (pbuh), O Muhammad (pbuh), Peace and blessings
of Allah (AJ) be upon you, O our Master Prophet Muhammad (pbuh)

(أَلْفِ صَلِّي الله عَلَيْكَ، يَا مُحَمَّدْ) x٢   (صَلَوَاتُ الله عَلَيْكَ سَيِّدْ مُحَمَّدْ) x٢

(Alfi SalAllah 'Alayka, YA MUHAMMAD) x2
(Salawatullah 'Alayka Sayyid Muhammad) x2

Thousand of Allah's (AJ) blessings be upon you, O Prophet Muhammad (pbuh), Peace
and blessings of Allah (AJ) be upon you, Master Muhammad (pbuh)

(يَا رَسُولَ الله يَامُحَمَّدْ، يَامُحَمَّدْ) x٢   (صَلَوَاتُ الله عَلَيْكَ سَيِّدْ مُحَمَّدْ) x٢

(Ya Rasul Allah Ya Muhammad, YA MUHAMMAD) x2
(Salawatullah 'Alayka Sayyid Muhammad) x2

O Messenger of Allah (AJ), O Prophet Muhammad (pbuh), Peace and blessings of
Allah (AJ) be upon you, Master Muhammad (pbuh)

(يَا حَبِيبَ الله يَا مُحَمَّدْ، يَامُحَمَّد) x٢   (صَلَوَاتُ الله عَلَيْكَ سَيِّدْ مُحَمَّدْ) x٢

(Ya Habib Allah Ya Muhammad, YA MUHAMMAD) x2
(Salawatullah 'Alayka Sayyid Muhammad) x2

O Beloved of Allah (AJ), O Prophet Muhammad (pbuh), Peace and blessings of Allah
(AJ) be upon you, Master Muhammad (pbuh)

(يَا نَبِي الله يَا مُحَمَّدْ، يَامُحَمَّد) x٢   (صَلَوَاتُ الله عَلَيْكَ سَيِّدْ مُحَمَّدْ) x٢

(Ya Nabi Allah Ya Muhammad, YA MUHAMMAD) x2
(Salawatullah 'Alayka Sayyid Muhammad) x2

O Prophet of Allah (AJ), O Prophet Muhammad (pbuh), Peace and blessings of Allah
(AJ) be upon you, Master Muhammad (pbuh)

(يَا خَلِيْلَ الله يَا مُحَمَّدْ، يَامُحَمَّدْ) x٢   (صَلَوَاتُ الله عَلَيْكَ سَيِّدْ مُحَمَّدْ) x٢

(Ya Khalil Allah Ya Muhammad, YA MUHAMMAD) x2
(Salawatullah 'Alayka Sayyid Muhammad) x2

O Friend of Allah (AJ), O Prophet Muhammad (pbuh), Peace and blessings of Allah (AJ)
be upon you, Master Muhammad (pbuh)

(يَا صَفِيُّ الله يَا مُحَمَّدْ، يَامُحَمَّدْ) x٢   (صَلَوَاتُ الله عَلَيْكَ سَيِّدْ مُحَمَّدْ) x٢

(Ya Safi Allah Ya Muhammad, YA MUHAMMAD) x2
(Salawatullah 'Alayka Sayyid Muhammad) x2

O intimate friend of Allah (AJ), O Prophet Muhammad (pbuh), Peace and blessings of
Allah (AJ) be upon you, Master Muhammad (pbuh)

(يَا نَجِّيُّ الله يَا مُحَمَّدْ، يَامُحَمَّدْ) x٢   (صَلَوَاتُ الله عَلَيْكَ سَيِّدْ مُحَمَّدْ) x٢

(Ya Najji Allah Ya Muhammad, YA MUHAMMAD) x2
(Salawatullah 'Alayka Sayyid Muhammad) x2

O Confidant of Allah (AJ), O Prophet Muhammad (pbuh), Peace and blessings of Allah
(AJ) be upon you, Master Muhammad (pbuh)

(يَا شَفِيْع الله يَا مُحَمَّدْ، يَامُحَمَّدْ) x٢   (صَلَوَاتُ الله عَلَيْكَ سَيِّدْ مُحَمَّدْ) x٢

(Ya Shafi' Allah Ya Muhammad, YA MUHAMMAD) x2
(Salawatullah 'Alayka Sayyid Muhammad) x2

O Intercessor of Allah (AJ), O Prophet Muhammad (pbuh), Peace and blessings of Allah
(AJ) be upon you, Master Muhammad (pbuh)

اَللّٰهُمَّ صَلِّ وَ سَلِّمْ وَ بَارِكْ عَلَيْهِ وَ عَلَي اَلِهْ
Allahuma salli wa sallim wa barik 'alayhi wa 'ala alih
O Allah (AJ) send peace and blessings upon Prophet Muhammad (pbuh) and his family.

Rabbi Faghfir li Dhunubi

رَبِّي فَأَغْفِرْليْ ذِنُوْبِيْ

بِبَرْكَةِ الْهَادِيْ مُحَمَّدْ ، يَا الله ‏ ‏ ‏ ‏ ‏ ‏ (رَبِّي فَأَغْفِرْليْ ذِنُوْبِيْ، يَا الله‏x۲

**(Rabbi faghfir li dhunubi Ya Allah
Bi barkatil Hadi Muhammad Ya Allah) x2**

O my Lord, forgive my sins, O Allah (AJ),
By the blessings of the Perfected guide, Prophet Muhammad (pbuh), O Allah (AJ)

فِيْ جِوَارِه خَيْرَ مَقْعَدْ، يَا الله ‏ ‏ ‏ ‏ ‏ ‏ رَبِّي بَلِغْنَا بِجَاهِهْ، يَا الله

**Rabbi balighna bi jahi, ya Allah
Fi jiwari khayra maq'ad, ya Allah**

O my Lord, let us reach (our destination), for the sake of Prophet Muhammad's (pbuh)
high station (with You), In his proximity is the best place to stay

CHORUS

أَشْرَفَ الرُّسْلِ مُحَمَّدْ، يَا الله ‏ ‏ ‏ ‏ ‏ ‏ وَصَلَاةَ اللهِ تَغْشَى، يَا الله

**Wa salatullahi taghsha, Ya Allah
Ashrafar Rusli Muhammad, Ya Allah**

May Allah's (AJ) blessings shower him, Prophet Muhammad (pbuh) is the noblest of the
Messengers

CHORUS

كُلَّ حِينٍ يَا تَجَدَّدْ، يَا الله ‏ ‏ ‏ ‏ ‏ ‏ وَسَلَامٌ مُسْتَمِرٌّ، يَا الله

**Wa salamun mustamirrun, Ya Allah
Kulla hinin ya tajaddad, Ya Allah**

Peace be upon him, Prophet Muhammad (pbuh), Continuously and renewed at every
moment

CHORUS

يَا رَسُوْلُ اللهِ أَهْلاً، يَا الله   بِكَ إِنَا بِكَ نُسْعَدْ، يَا الله

Ya Rasulullahi ahlan, Ya Allah
Bika inna bika nus'ad, Ya Allah

Welcome O Messenger of Allah (AJ) Welcome, For verily with you is our joy and happiness

CHORUS

جُدْ وَ بَلِّغْ كُلَّ مَقْصَدْ، يَا الله   وَ بِجَاهِهٖ يَا إِلَهِيْ، يَا الله

Wa bijahi, ya ilahi, Ya Allah
Jud wa balligh kulla maqsad, Ya Allah

And by Prophet Muhammad's (pbuh) high honored station, O our Lord,
Give us generously and grant us all that we are in need of

CHORUS

كَيْ بِهٖ نُسْعَدْ وَنُرْشَدْ، يَا الله   وَاهْدِنَا نَهْجَ سَبِيْلِهٖ، يَا الله

Wahdina nahja sabilih, Ya Allah
Kay bihi nus'ad wa nurshad, Ya Allah

Guide us with his methods and directions, O Allah (AJ),
So that we receive happiness and guidance, O Allah (AJ)

CHORUS

اَللّٰهُمَّ صَلِّ وَ سَلِّمْ وَ بَارِكْ عَلَيْهِ وَ عَلَي آلِهْ
Allahuma salli wa sallim wa barik 'alayhi wa 'ala alih
O Allah (AJ) send peace and blessings upon Prophet Muhammad (pbuh) and his family.

Lama Nadani Huwa
لَمَا نَادَانِيْ هُو

فَصِرْتُ عَبْدًا مَمْلُوْكًا لَهُ هُو) x۲   (اَللهُ اَلله، لَمَا نَادَانِيْ هُوَ

(Allahu Allah, lama nadani Huwa   **Fasirtu 'abdan, mamlukan lahu Huwa) x2**

When Allah (AJ) called His beloved messenger, "Huwa" (the Heness). I (Muhammad (pbuh)) became the servant of the Lord Almighty, Owned by the Sovereign King of all creation, "Huwa" (the Unknown Essence of the Divine)

مَا أَنْتَ إِلَّا كَنْزُ الْعَطِيَّة   خَيْرِ الْبَرِيَّة، نَظْرَة إِلَيَّ

Khairil bariyah, nazhra ilayya   **Ma anta illa, kanzul 'atiyah**

O the best of creation (Prophet Muhammad (pbuh)), gaze upon me, You are the treasure that Allah (AJ) has send as a blessing and Mercy to Creation

جُدْلِيْ بِوَصْلٍ، قَبْلَ الْمَنِيَّة   يَا بَحْرُ فَضْلٍ، وَتَاجَ عَدْلٍ

Ya bahro fadlin, wa taaja 'adlin   **Judli bi waslin, qablal maniya**

O (Prophet Muhammad (pbuh)), You are the ocean of all bounty and emanations, you are the crown of Justice, Please expedite my union to your beautiful light, and let me reunite with you before my passing

CHORUS

يَكْفِيْ عِبَادِيْ، يَا نُوْرُ عَيْنِيًا   كَمْ ذَا أُنَادِيْ، يَاخَيْرُ هَادِيْ

Kamdha unadi, ya khairo Hadi   **Yakfi 'ibadi, ya Nooro 'ainiya**

I keep calling upon you, O the best of guides, You are the complete and perfected servant of Allah (AJ), O the light of my eyes/vision

يَاخَيْرُ مُرْسَلْ، إِرْحَمْ شَجِيَّة   حَاشَاكَ تَغْفُلْ عَنَّا وَتَبْخُلْ

Hashaka taghful, 'anna wa tabkhul   **Ya khairo mursal, irham shajiya**

Glory be to you above all, You can ignore us or withhold from us your mercy, O the best of messengers, don't overlook me, have mercy and pity upon my soul and gaze upon me

CHORUS

إِنِّيْ مُحِبٌّ، بِذِكْرِ اَحْمَدْ   بَشِّرْ مُحِبًّا، وَلَوْ بِرُؤْيَا

Inni muhibbun, bi dhikri Ahmad   **Bashir muhibban, walau biRuya**

I am in love with the remembrance and praising of Prophet Ahmad (Muhammad (pbuh)), Give the good news to those who love you O our Master Muhammad (pbuh), even if it is through a dream

مَادَامَ قَلْبِيْ، بِالذِّكْرِ حَيَّ   اُهْدِيْكَ حُبِّيْ، صَلَاةَ رَبِّيْ

Uhdika hubbi, salatu Rabbi   **Madama qalbi, bidh-dhikri Hayya**

I present to you my love through God's prayers and blessings upon you [Salawat], As long as my heart is in remembrance of Hayy, the ocean of Ever-living and eternity

CHORUS

عِنْدَ الصَّبَاحِ مَعَ الْعَشِيَّة   كَذَا سَلَامِيْ، عَلَىَ الدَّوَامِ

Kadha Salami, 'aladDawami   **'Indas sabahi, ma'al 'ashiyah**

Also, peace be upon you O Prophet Muhammad (pbuh) eternally, From morning through the nighttime

مَاطَابَ عَيْشِيْ وَ لَا وُجُوْدِيْ   لَوْ لَاكَ يَا، زِيْنَةَ الْوُجُوْدِ

Laulaka yaa, zinatal wujudi   **Ma taba 'aishi, wa la wujudi**

If it were not for you (O Muhammad (pbuh)), I would not have had a life or existence, Your light is the beauty and honour in our existence

CHORUS

وَ لَا رُكُوْعِيْ وَ لَا سُجُوْدِيْ   وَ لَا تَرْنَمْتَ، فِىْ صَلَاتِيْ

Wa la tarnamtu, fi Salati   **Wa la ruku'yi, wa la sujudi**

If it were not for your love, I would not have chanted your beautiful name, in my prayers, Nor in my kneeling nor in my prostration

عُوْدِئ لِيْحَضْرُ، مِنْكَ عُوْدِئ   أَيَا لَيَالِي الرِّضَا عَلَيْنَا

Aya layalir, rida 'alaina   **'Odi lihadru, minka 'Odi**

O My Lord we seek your satisfaction, Allow us to be in your holy presence
O Prophet Muhammad (pbuh), let us to return back to your divinely light

CHORUS

بِالْمُصْطَفَى، طَيِّبُ الْجُدُودِ   عُوْدِئْ عَلَيْنَا، بِكُلِّ خَيْرٍ

'Odi 'alayna, bikulli khairin   **Bil Mustafa, Tayibul jududi**

Let your holy presence come to us with all the goodness, By the chosen one who has the purest of ancestors

فَإِنَّ شَوْقِىْ، لَكُمْ يَزِيْدُوْا   بِاللهِ عِيْدُوا، وصَالِ عِيْدُوْا

Billahi 'Eidu wisali 'Eidu   **Fa inna shawqi lakum yazidu**

For the grace of God, return us back to our origin, My longing for you Prophet Muhammad (pbuh) has been increasing, please reunite me with your beautiful light

CHORUS

فَإِنَّ يَوْمَ ، وصَالِ عِيْدُ   وَجَدِّدُوْا، كُلَّ يَوْم وَصْلِ

Wa jaddidu, kulla yaumi wasli   **Fa inna yauma wisali 'Eidu**

And my connection with you is renewed every day, And the day I go back to my origin and I am reunited with you, would be the day of Eid (celebration)

وَقَلِّبُوْهُ ، كَمَا تُرِيْدُوْا   خُذُوْا فُؤَادِئْ، وَفَتِّشُوْهُ

Khudhu fuadi, wa fattishuhu   **Wa qallibohu, kama turidu**

Take my heart and search through it, And purify it and guide it as you wish

CHORUS

عَلَيَّ زِيْدُوا الْبِعَادَ زِيْدُوْا   فَإِنْ وَجَدْتُمْ فِيْهِ سِوَاكُمْ

Fa in wajadtum, fihi siwakum   **'Alayya zidul bi'ada zidu**

If you found anyone except you inside my heart, cleanse it and don't allow it to create a distance from you. O my beloved, don't let my heart to be distant from you

وَآلِهِ الرُّكَّعِ السُّجُوْدِ   ثَمَّ الصَّلَاةُ عَلَى نَبِيِّنَا

Thummas salatu 'ala Nabiyina   **Wa alihi Rukka'is sujudi**

At the end, blessing be upon our Prophet Muhammad (pbuh) and his holy family, Peace be upon them especially in my kneeling and prostrations

CHORUS

Part D
Urdu Nasheeds

Jashne Aamade Rasul

جشنِ آمدِ رسول

(Celebration of the Arrival of the Messenger)

(بی بی آمنہ کے پھو ل اللہ ہی اللہ)x۲   (جشنِ آمدِ رسول اللہ ہی اللہ)x۲

(Jashne aamade Rasul, Allahi Allah) x2
(Bibi Amina ke pool, Allahi Allah) x2

Celebrate the Arrival of the Messenger (Prophet Muhammad (pbuh)), the flower of the beloved Amina (Prophet Muhammad's (pbuh) mother)

جشنِ آمدِ رسول اللہ ہی اللہ   (اللہ ہی اللہ بولو اللہ ہی اللہ)x۲

(Allahi Allah bolo Allahi Allah) x2
Jashne aamade Rasul Allahi Allah

Say Allah and celebrate the arrival of the
Messenger of Allah (Prophet Muhammad (pbuh))

جبکہ سرکار تشریف لانے لگے
حور وِغلماں بھی خوشیاں منانے لگے
ہر طرف نور کی روشنی چھا گئ
مصطفیٰ کیا ملے زندگی مل گئ

Jab ke sarkaar tashreef lane lagee
Hoor o ghilma bhi khushayaa mananay lagee
Har taraf noor ki, Roshni chaa gayee
Mustafa kya melee, zindagi mil gayee

(اے حلیمہ تری گود میں آ گیا)x۲
(دونوں عالم کے رسول اللہ ہی اللہ)x۲
(اللہ ہی اللہ بولو اللہ ہی اللہ)x۲

(Eh Halima teri goad may aa gayea) x2
(Dono aalam ke Rasul, Allahi Allah) x2
(Allahi Allah, bolo Allahi Allah) x2

When the Master arrived, the Hurain and Ghulams – Angels of Paradise celebrated with happiness. His holy light illuminated everywhere, With the arrival of the Chosen One, we were given life/existence. O Halima (Prophet's wet nurse), you received in your lap, the Messenger of both worlds.

CHORUS

چہرہِ مصطفیٰ جب دیکھایا گیا

جُھک گئیے تارے اور چاند شرما گیا

آمنہ دیکھ کر مسکرانے لگیں

حوا مریم بھی خوشیاں منانے لگیں

Chehra e Mustafa jab dikaya gaya
Jhuk gaye taare, Or chaand Sharma gaya
Amina dekh kar, muskuraane lagee
Hawa Maryam bhi, khushiya manaane lagee

(آمنہ بی بی سب سے یہ کہنے لگیں) x۲

(دعا ہو گئی قبول اللہ ہی اللہ) x۲

(اللہ ہی اللہ بولو اللہ ہی اللہ) x۲

(Amina bib sab say yeh kehne lagee) x2
(Dua ho gayee qabool, Allahi Allah) x2
(Allahi Allah, bolo Allahi Allah) x2

When the holy face of Mustafa was unveiled, Stars bowed down and the Moon became shy, Amina saw him and started to smile, Hawa (Eve) and Maryam (Mary) (who were spiritually present with Amina (as)) also celebrated with happiness. Amina said to everyone, "My prayer has been accepted"

CHORUS

شادیانے خوشی کے بجائے گئے

شادی کے نغمے سب کو سنائے گئے

ہر طرف شور صلی علیٰ ہو گیا

آج پیدا حبیبِ خدا ہو گیا

Shadiyaane khushi ke bajaaye gayeh
Shaadi ke naghme sab ko sunaaye gayeh
Har taraf shore Salli ala ho gaya
Aaj payda Habibe khuda hogaya

(پھر تو جبرایل نے بھی یہ علاں کیا)x۲
(یہ خدا کے ہیں رسول اللہ ہی اللہ)x۲
(اللہ ہی اللہ بولو اللہ ہی اللہ)x۲

(Pihr to Jibril ne bhi ye eilaan kiya) x2
(Yea khuda ke hai Rasul, Allahi Allah) x2
(Allahi Allah, bolo Allahi Allah) x2

Music of happiness was played everywhere, Poems of happiness were recited for everyone, Everywhere were the shouts of Salli Ala (praising be upon him), Today the Beloved of Allah (AJ) is born, Then Gabriel announced to everyone, this is the Messenger of Allah (AJ)

CHORUS

Shahe Madina

شاہِ مدینہ

(The King of Medina)

(شاہِ مدینہ ، شاہِ مدینہ)x۲
طیبہ کے والی، سارے نبی تیرے در کے سوالی

(Shahe Madina, Shahe Madina) x2
Tayba ke waali, Saare Nabi terey dar ke sawali
O Sultan of Madina, O Sultan Of Madina

The King of Madina (city of light), The Protector of good,
All the prophets seek answers at your door, O King of Madina

تیرے لیے ہی، دنیا بنی ہے
(نیلے فلک کی، چادر تنی ہے)x۲

(تو اگر نہ ہوتا)x۲   دنیا تھی خالی
سارے نبی تیرے در کے سوالی

Terey liyea hee, Dunya bani hay
(Neelay falak ki, Chadar tani hay) x2
(Tu agar na hota) x2,   Dunya thi khali
Saare nabi tere dar ke sawali

The universe is created for you, the blue sheet of the sky is spread out for you, If you were
not in existence, the world would have been empty, All prophets are at your door
seeking help

CHORUS

تو نے جہاں کی محفل سجائ
(تاریکیوں میں شمع جلائ)x۲

(ہر سمت چھائ)x۲   رات کالی
سارے نبی تیرے در کے سوالی

Tuney jahaa ke mehfil sajayee
(Tarikiyo may shama jalayee) x2
(Har semt chayee) x2,   Raat kalee
Sarey Nabi teri dar ki sawali

You adorned the assembly/gathering of this world. Your holy light is a bright torch that illuminated the darkness that had spread everywhere in the world. All prophets are at your door seeking help.

CHORUS

جلوے ہیں سارے ، تیرے ہی دم سے
(آباد عالم ،تیرے کرم سے)x۲
(باقی ہر اِک شے)x۲   نقشِ خیالی
سارے نبی تیرے در کے سوالی

**Jalwey hai saare, Terey hi dam say
(Aabad aalam, Terey karam say) x2
(Baqi har eyk shay) x2,   Naqshe khayali
Saare nabi tere dar ke sawali**

All beauty is from your beauty, The world is in existence due to your blessings and mercy (you are a mercy to creation), Everything else is nothing but an imaginary picture, All prophets are at your door seeking help

CHORUS

ہے نور تیرا شمس و قمر میں
(تیرے لبوں کی لا لی سحر میں)x۲
(پھولوں نے تیری)x۲   خوشبو چُرا لی
سارے نبی تیرے در کے سوالی

**Hay Noor tera shams o qamar may
(Tere labo ki, Laali sahar may) x2
(Poolo ne Teri) x2,   Khushbu chura li
Saare Nabi tere dar ke sawali**

Your light is in the Sun and the Moon, The dawn has the redness of your holy lips, All flowers have stolen your fragrance, All prophets are at your door seeking help

CHORUS

مزہب ہے تیرا ، سب کی بھلای
(مَسلک ہے تیرا ، مشکل کُشائ)x۲
(دیکھ اپنی امت کی)x۲   خَستہ حالی
سارے نبی تیرے در کے سوالی

Mazhab hay tera, Sab ki bhalayee
(Maslak hai tera, Mushkil Kushayee) x2
(Dekh apni umat ki) x2,   Khasta haali,
Sare nabi tere dar ke sawali

Wanting good for everyone is your religion, Making all difficulties disappear is what you do, Gaze upon your tired/helpless nation

CHORUS

Noor Wala Aaya Hay

نور والا آیا ہے

(The Owner of Light Has Arrived)

(نور والا آیا ہے ,نور لے کر آیا ہے) x۲
سارے عالم میں یہ دیکھو، کیسا نور چھایا ہے
(اصلاۃ وسلام و علیکَ یا رسول الله
اصلاۃ وسلام و علیکَ یا حبیب الله)x۲

(Noor wala aya hay, Noor lay kar aya hay) x2
Sare alam may yea dekho, Kaisa noor chaya hay
(As Sallatu Was Salamu 'Alayka Ya RasulAllah
As Sallatu Was Salamu, 'Alayka Ya HabibAllah) x2

The Owner of the light (Prophet Muhammad (pbuh)) has arrived,
He has brought light with him,
Look how he has spread light in the entire universe
Peace and Blessings be upon you, O Messenger of Allah (AJ)
Peace and Blessings be upon you, O Beloved of Allah (AJ)

(جب تلک یہ چاند تارے جھلملاتے جائیں گے
تب تلک جشنِ ولادت ہم مناتے جائیں گے)x۲

(Jab talak yeh chand taare, Jhil meelate jayengay
Tab talak jashney wiladat, Hum manate jayengay) x2

Till the light of the moon and the stars shine in the world,
We will be comemmorating the celebration of His Holy Birth

CHORUS

(نعتِ محبوبِ خدا، سنتے سناتے جائیں گے
یا رسول الله کا نعرہ لگاتے جائیں گے)x۲

(Naate mehboobe khuda, Sunte sunatay jayengay
Ya RasulAllah ka, Nara lagatay jayengay) x2

We will be singing and letting others hear, the poems of love and praising of the Beloved
of Allah (AJ), We will be shouting the slogan of
"Ya RasulAllah" (O Messenger of Allah (AJ))

CHORUS

(چہار جانب ہم دیے گھی کے ،جلاتے جائیں گے

گھر تو گھر سارے محلے کو ،سجاتے جائیں گے)x۲

(Chaar janeb hum diyea ghee kay, Jalatay jayengay
Ghar tu ghar, sarey mohalle ko, Sajatay jayengay) x2

We will be lighting lamps of oil in all corners everywhere,
We will decorate, not only our homes but the entire city with lights

CHORUS

(عید میلادالنبی کی شب چراغاں کر کے ہم

قبر، نورِ مصطفیٰ سے جگمگاتے جائیں گے)x۲

(Eid e Miladun Nabi ki shab, Charagha kar kay hum
Qabr, Noore Mustafa say, Jagmagatay jayengay) x2

We will light up the night with torches on the eve of the Birth of Prophet Muhammad
(pbuh), that will make our graves bright with the light of Chosen One

CHORUS

(تم کرو جشنِ ولادت کی، خوشی میں روشنی

وہ تمہاری گورِ تیرا جگمگاتے جائیں گے)x۲

(Tum karo Jashney Wiladat ki, Kushi may roshini
Woh tumhari gor e teera, Jagmagate jayengay) x2

You light up candles in the happiness and celebration of His Holy Birth,
He (pbuh) will fill your dark grave with bright and shining light

CHORUS

Ya Mustafa

يا مصطفیٰ

(O Chosen One)

۴x (یا مصطفیٰ، یا مصطفیٰ)

(Ya Mustafa, Ya Mustafa) x4

O Chosen One, O Chosen One

تو ہے عاشقِ نبی، سب کو یہ بتائے جا

مصطفیٰ کے عشق میں محفلیں سجائے جا

(جشنِ آمدِ نبی) x۲

(دل سے تو منائے جا) x۲

Tu hay aashiqe Nabi, sab ko yeh bataye jaa

Mustafa kay ishq may, Mehfiley sajaye jaa

(Jashney aamade Nabi) x2

(Dil say tu manaye jaa) x2

You are a Lover of Prophet Muhammad (pbuh), Tell it to everyone! In his love, keep putting up events of celebration for the love of the Chosen One, Celebrate the arrival of Prophet wholeheartedly in a Grand Way, and Say, O Chosen One, (Muhammad (pbuh))

CHORUS

دامنِ نبی پکڑ اور خدا کا نام لے

پرچمِ نبی کو تو آگے بڑھ کے تھام لے

(نعرہِ محمدی) x۲

(زور سے لگائے جا) x۲

Damane Nabi pakar, Or Khuda ka naam lay

Parchame Nabi ko tu, Aagey barh kay tham lay

(Nara e Muhammadi) x2

(Zor say lagaye jaa) x2

Hold tight to the cloak of Prophet Muhammad (pbuh) and mention God's name
Hold the Flag of Prophet (pbuh) and move forward,
Shout the slogan of Muhammadi, with a loud voice!

CHORUS

گفتگو کی ابتدا، کر تو لفظ تول کر
دل سبھی کا جیت لے میٹھے بول بول کر
(جن سے تجھ کو عشق ہے) x۲
(ان کے گیت گائے جا) x۲

Guftugu ki ibteda, Kar tu lafz tol kar
Dil sabhi ka jeet lay, Meethay bol bol kar
(Jin say tujh ko ishq hay) x2
(Un kay geet gaye jaa) x2

Start the conversation by weighing your words carefully, Win everyone's heart by speaking sweet words, Keep singing the songs of the ones whom you love

CHORUS

مرشدی کی بات کو، اپنے پلے باندھ لے
سامنے جو آئیں وہ، اُن کو ہاتھوں ہاتھ لے
(اونچا رُتبہ پا کے تو) x۲
(مرتبہ بڑھا ئے جا) x۲

Murshedi ki baat ko, Apnay pallay baandh lay
Samnay joo aayeh woh, Un ko hatho hath lay
(Oocha rutbah paa kay tu) x2
(Martaba barhaay jaa) x2

Listen carefully and hold tight to the advice of your Shaykh (Spiritual Guide), If he comes in front of you, grab his hands with respect, By respecting and listening to advice/teachings of your shaykh, you will attain a high spiritual station and move up to even higher stations

CHORUS

باغوں میں بہشت کے ،رات دن تو گھوما کر
اپنے والدین کے، ہاتھ پاؤں چوما کر
(بخت کو جگائے جا) x۲
(دل میں گھر بنائے جا) x۲

Bagho may bahesht kay, Raat din tu ghooma kar
Apnay waledain kay, Haath pao chooma kar
(Bakht ko jagaye jaa) x2
(Dil may ghar banaye jaa) x2

Roam in the gardens of heaven day and night; Kiss the hands and feet of your parents (out of respect), Awake your destiny by making a house in their hearts

CHORUS

پیار کر تو بچوں سے، عزتیں بڑوں کی کر

دامنِ مراد کو، اپنے تو دعا سے بھر

x۲ (سیرتِ نبی سے تو)

x۲ (فائدہ اٹھائے جا)

Pyar kar to bacho say, Izzatai baro ki kar,
Damane murad ko, Apnay tu dua say bhar
(Seerate Nabi say tu) x2
(Faida uthaye jaa) x2

Love the kids and respect the elders, Fill your bowl of desires Fill your spiritual account with prayers and good wishes from others, Learn and benefit from the Virtue/ Way of Prophet (pbuh) in your life

CHORUS

یومِ مصطفیٰ تجھے اب کے یوں منانا ہے

سبز پرچموں سے گھر، خوب تر سجانا ہے

x۲ (جشنِ آمدِ نبی)

x۲ (دل سے تو منائے جا)

Yawme Mustafa tujhay, Ab kay you manana hay
Sabz parchamo say ghar, Khoob tar sajana hay
(Jashney aamade Nabi) x2
(Dil say tu manaye jaa) x2

From now on, this is how you celebrate Prophet Muhammad's Birthday! Decorate the house with beautiful green flags, celebrate the arrival of Prophet (pbuh) wholeheartedly in a Grand way

CHORUS

Is Karam ka Karo Shukr Kaisey

اِس کرم کا کروں شکر کیسے

(How Do I Thank You for this Generosity?)

(اس کرم کا کروں ،شکر کیسے ادا) x۲
جو کرم مجھ پہ ،میرے نبی کر دیا

(Is karam ka karo, shukr kaisey ada) x2
Jo karam mujh pey, merey Nabi kar diya

How do I show my gratitude for this generosity? The generosity that my Prophet Muhammad (pbuh) has bestowed upon me.

(میں سجاتا تھا ،سرکار کی محفلیں) x۲
مجھ کو ہر غم سے ،رب نے بری کر دیا

(May sajata tha, Sarkaar ki mehfiley) x2
Mujh ko har gham se, Rab ne bari kar diya

I kept organizing events of celebration for Prophet's (pbuh) holy birth and his presence on this earth. And my Lord freed me from all the sadness and difficulties in here and hereafter

(ذکرِ سرکار کی ،ہیں بڑی برکتیں) x۲
مل گئیں راحتیں ،عظمتیں رفعتیں
(میں گناہ گار تھا ،بے عمل تھا مگر) x۲
مصطفیٰ نے مجھے ،جنتی کر دیا

(Zikre sarkaar ki, hay bari barkatey) x2
Mil gayi rahatey, azmatey rifatey
(May gunahgaar tha, bey amal tha magar) x2
Mustafa ney mujhe, Jannati kar diya

There is an immense blessing in remembrance and praising of the Master of both worlds through which we have found peace, contentment, honour and high stations. I was a sinner and had no good deeds, but the Chosen One, Prophet Muhammad (pbuh), made me from the people of heavens.

CHORUS

(لمحہ لمحہ ہے ،مجھ پر نبی کی عطا) x۲

دوستوں اور مانگوں ،میں مولا سے کیا

(کیا یہ کم ہے کہ ،میرے خدا نے مجھے) x۲

اپنے محبوب کا ،اُمتی کر دیا

(Lamha lamha hay, mujh par Nabi ki ata) x2
Dosto or mango, may Mawla sey kya?
(Kya yeh kam hay ke, merey Khuda ne mujhe) x2
Apni mehboob ka, ummati kar diya

At every moment, I am in debt to Prophet's (pbuh) generosity and blessings. O my friends, what else can I ask from my Lord? Is it not enough honour that my God made me to be from the nation of His Beloved Prophet Muhammad (pbuh)?

(جو درِ مصطفٰی کے ،گدا ہو گیے) x۲

دیکھتے دیکھتے ،کیا سے کیا ہو گیے

(ایسی چشمِ کرم ،کی ہے سرکار نے) x۲

دونوں عالم میں، اُن کو غنی کر دیا

(Jo dar e Mustafa ke, gada ho gayea) x2
Daykhtey daykhtey, kya se kya ho gayea
(Aisee chashme karam, ki hey sarkaar ney) x2
Dono aalam ne, un ko ghani kar diya

Whomever came to the door of the Chosen One (pbuh) as a poor, needy orphan, look how far they have come and what they have achieved. When the immensely generous gaze of the Prophet (pbuh) fell upon them, he (pbuh) enriched them by his generosity in both worlds.

CHORUS

(کوئی مایوس لوٹا ،نہ دربار سے) x۲

جو بھی مانگا، ملا میرے سرکار سے

(صدقے جاؤں نیازی میں لجپال کے) x۲

ہر گدا کو، سخی نے سخی کر دیا

(Koyi mayos lauta, na darbar sey) x2
Jo bhi manga, mila mere sarkar sey
(Sadqe jawoo 'Niyazi', may lajpal key) x2
Har gada ko, sakhi ne sakhi kar diya

Nobody has ever returned hopeless from the kingdom of Prophet Muhammad (pbuh). Whatever they asked for, they received from our Master. May I be sacrificed for such an honourable master; the Generous servant of Allah (AJ), whom made every poor person to become generous.

(اس کرم کا کروں ،شکر کیسے ادا) x۲
جو کرم مجھ پہ میرے نبی کر دیا
(میں سجاتا تھا ،سرکار کی محفلیں) x۲
مجھ کو ہر غم سے ،رب نے بری کر دیا

(Is karam ka karo, shukr kaisey ada) x2
Jo karam mujh pe mere nabi kar diya
(May sajata tha, Sarkaar ki mehfiley) x2
Mujh ko har gham se, Rab ne bari kar diya

How do I show my gratitude for this generosity? The generosity that my Prophet Muhammad (pbuh) has bestowed upon me. I kept organizing events of celebration for Prophet's (pbuh) holy birth and his presence on this earth. And my Lord freed me from all the sadness and difficulties in here and hereafter

CHORUS

The Green Dome of Madina

(فاصلوں کو تکلف ہے ہم سے اگر

ہم بھی بے بس نہیں بے سہارا نہیں)x۲

(Faselo ko takalluf hai hum se agar
Hum bhi bebas nahi be sahara nahi) x2

If distances prove themselves to be pretentious towards us
We are neither helpless, nor without support

جیسے ہی سبز گنبد نظر آئے گا

بندگی کا قرینہ بدل جائے گا

Jaise hee sabz Gunbad nazar ayega
Bandagi ka qareena badal jayega

The moment the Green Dome becomes visible, the nature of Servanthood will change

(When the green dome of Madina comes in to my sight) x2
(The whole of Dunya is buried in its light) x2

CHORUS

ہم مدینے میں تنہا نکل جائیں گے

اور گلیوں میں قصدَن بھٹک جائیں گے

ہم وہاں جا کے واپس نہیں آئیں گے

ڈھونڈتے ڈھونڈتے ,لوگ تھک جائیں گے

Hum Madinay may tanha nikal jayengay
Or galiyo may kasdan bhatak jayengay
Ham vahaa jaake vaapas nahi ayengay
Dhoond te dhoond te, log thak jayengay

We will go out alone in Madina, And deliberately lose our way in its streets
Once we go there, we won't come back, People would get tired looking for us

The one for whom the universe was created in truth
Is reading Sakina beneath the Emerald Roof) x2

CHORUS

نامِ آقا جہاں بھی لیا جائے گا
ذکر اُن کا جہاں بھی کیا جائے گا
نور ہی نور سینوں میں بھر جائے گا
ساری محفل میں جلوے لپک جائیں گے

Naam e Aaqa jaha bhi liyaa jayega,
Zikr un ka jaha bhi kiyaa jayega
Noor hee noor seeno may bhar jayega
Saari mehfil may jalway lapak jaaengay

The Master's name (Prophet Muhammad (pbuh)), wherever it is mentioned,
Wherever his remembrance will be made, Light will fill up the hearts,
Spiritual manifestations will bless and shower the entire gathering/association

(His name, peace be upon him, is inscribed on the throne) x2
(What greater the honour than to visit his dome) x2
Than to visit His Dome
(The beautiful green Dome) x2

Mustafa Jaane Rehmat

مصطفیٰ جانِ رحمت

(The Chosen One, the Spirit of Mercy)

مصطفیٰ جانِ رحمت پہ، لاکھوں سلام

شمعِ بزمِ ہدایت پہ، لاکھوں سلام

Mustafa Jaane Rehmat pe, Laakho salaam
Shamme bazme hidayat pe, Laako salaam

Millions of blessings of peace be upon the Chosen One, the Spirit of Mercy, the Light of Guidance, Prophet Muhammad (pbuh)

نقطہء سرِ وحدت پہ یکتا درود

مرکزِ دورِ کثرت پہ لاکھوں سلام

Nuqta e sirre Wahdat pe, Yakta Durood
Markaze daure kasrat pe, Laakho salaam

Incomparable praising be upon the origin/base of the Secret of Oneness, Millions of salutations upon whom is the Center of Authority

اصلِ ہر بود و بہبودُ تخمِ وجود

قاسمِ کَنزِ نعمت پہ لاکھوں سلام

Asle har boodo, behboodo, Tukhme Wajood
Qasim e kanze ne'mat pe, Laakho salaam

He is the essence of every creation and the kernel of their existence. Millions of salutations be upon the Distributor of Treasures of Divine's blessings

CHORUS

شَرقِ انوارِ قدرت پہ نوری درود

فاتحِ اظہارِ قدرت پہ لاکھوں سلام

Sharqe Anwaare Qudrat pe, Noori Durood
Fathe AzHaare Qurbat pe, Laakho salaam

Luminous praising be upon the first light created and the root and beginning of all creation. Millions of salutations be upon the Opener of the Manifestation of Divine Nearness

وصف جس کا ہے آئینہِ حق نما
اُس خدا ساز طلعت پہ لاکھوں سلام

Wasf jiska hay, Aayina e haqnuma
Us Khuda saaz tal'at pe, Laakho salaam

The one with the highest honour, whose attribute is the mirror of Allah (AJ), Millions of salutations be upon his Holy Face that can create such a majestic divine reflection

CHORUS

عرش کی زیب و زینت پہ عرشی درود
فرش کی طِیب و نزہت پہ لاکھوں سلام

Arsh ki zebo zeenat pe, Arshi Durood
Farsh ki teebo nuzhat pe, Laakho salaam

Heavenly praising upon the one who is the Ornament of Heavens. Millions of salutations upon whom is the purity and fragrance of the earth. The earth was made habitable and beautiful because he would walk on it

CHORUS

جس کے گھیرے میں ہیں انبیا و ملک
اُس جہانگیرِ بعثت پہ لاکھوں سلام

Jiske gehere me hay, Anbiya O Malak
Us Jahangeer e ba'sat pe, Laakho salaam

In whose circle are the Prophets and Angels, Millions of salutations be upon the Conqueror of the World that has such a vast reach

عرش تا فرش ہے جس کے زیرِ نگیں
اس کی قاہر ریاست پہ لاکھوں سلام

Arsh taa Farsh hay, jiske zere nagee
Uski qaahir riyasat pe, Laakho salaam

From Heavens to Earth, everything is under his authority, Millions of salutations be upon his Victorious Kingdom

CHORUS

Partave isme zaate ahad par, Durood
Nushka e jaamiyat pe, Laakho salaam

Blessings be upon whom is the radiating light and reflection of the holy name of Al Ahad (Oneness). Millions of salutations be upon whom is the Complete Manuscript, the holy Quran

وہ دہن جس کی ہر بات وحئ خدا
چشمہءِ علم و حکمت پہ لاکھوں سلام

Woh daha jiski har baat, Wahye Khuda
Chashma e ilmo hikmat pe, Laakho salaam

Every word from his holy mouth is a Divine Revelation (Quran 53:3-4). Millions of salutations be upon his holy lips that is the source of Divine's knowledge and wisdom

CHORUS

دل سمجھ سے ورا ہے مگر یوں کہو
غنچہءِ رازِ وحدت پہ لاکھوں سلام

Dil samajh se waraa hay, magar yoo kahoo
Ghuncha e raaz e wahdat pe, Laakho salaam

The majesty of your holy heart is beyond my knowledge and understanding, but I would say this, Millions of salutations be upon the Rosebud holding the Secrets of Oneness!

صاحبِ رجعتِ شمس و شقُّ القمر
نائبِ دستِ قدرت پہ لاکھوں سلام

Sahibe rej'ate, Shamso shaqqul qamar
Nayib e daste qudrat pe, Laakho salaam

The Master who moved the sun to turn back the time, and split the moon with a sign of his finger. Millions of salutations be upon whom is the Deputy/Hand of the Divine's Power

CHORUS

جس طرف اُٹھ گئی دم میں دم آ گیا
اُس نگاہِ عنایت پہ لاکھوں سلام

Jiss taraf uth gayi, Dam may dam aa gaya
Us nigah e Inayat pe, Laakho salaam

Wherever he looked, the dead came to life and dead souls were revived, Millions of salutations be upon that Life-bestowing Gaze

کس کو دیکھا یہ موسیٰ سے پوچھے کوئی
آنکھوں والوں کی ہمت پہ لاکھوں سلام

Kis ko dekha, yeh Musa se pooche koyi
Aankho waalo ki himmat pe, Laakho salaam

Someone should ask Prophet Moses (as), Whom did he see? Millions of salutations upon the Courageous Eyes that could witness that glory

CHORUS

فتح بابِ نبوت پہ بےحد درود
ختمِ دورِ رسالت پہ لاکھوں سلام

Fathe baab e nubuvvat pe, Behad Durood
Khatme daur e risalat pe, Laakho salaam

Countless praises be upon whom is the Opener of the Door of Prophethood. Millions of salutations upon the Seal of the Prophets who ended the era of prophethood

جس کے ماتھے شفاعت کا سہرا رہا
اُس جبینِ سعادت پہ لاکھوں سلام

Jiske mathe shafa'at ka, Sehra raha
Us jabeen e sa'adat pe, Laakho salaam

On whose holy head is the Crown of Intercession, Millions of salutations be upon our Master's holy forehead, who will prostrate in the day of judgment to ask Allah (AJ) for our forgiveness

Ya RasulAllah (s) Marhaba Marhaba

یا رسول الله (ص) مرحبا مرحبا

(Welcome O Messenger of Allah)

(یا رسول الله ، مرحبا مرحبا
یا حبیب الله، مرحبا مرحبا)x۲

**(Ya RasulAllah, Marhaba Marhaba
Ya HabibAllah, Marhaba Marhaba) x2**

Welcome O Messenger of Allah (AJ), Prophet Muhammad (pbuh),
Welcome O Beloved of Allah (AJ), our Master Prophet Muhammad (pbuh)

بے کسوں سے ہے، جنہیں پیار، وہی آئے ہیں
دونوں عالم کے ہیں، غمخوار ،وہی آئے ہیں

**Bekaso se hay, jinhe pyar, Wohi aaye hay
Dono alam ke hay, ghamkhar, Wohi aaye hay**

The One who loves the helpless ones, has arrived,
The Comforter/Consoler of both worlds has arrived

CHORUS

اِک نظر آسماں پہ ڈال، مرحبا
چمکا ماہے نور کا حلال ,مرحبا

**Ek nazar aasma pe daal, Marhaba
Chamka mahe noor ka Hilal, Marhaba**

Look up to the sky once, Welcome the shining crescent of the "Month of Light"

CHORUS

جھنڈے لگاوئ ،گلیاں سجاوئ
کر لو چراغاں، گھر جگمگاوئ
راضی ہو گا ربِ ذولجلال, (مرحبا) x۲

**Jhande lagao, Galiya sajao
Karlo charagha, Ghar jagmagao
Razi hoga Rabbe Zuljalal, (Marhaba) x2**

Raise flags, decorate the streets, put on torches, Brighten the house for Celebration of his Birth, The Lord of Majesty will be pleased with you

CHORUS

محفل سجاؤ ،نعتیں سناؤ

آقا کی آمد کی، دوھمیں مچاؤ

روزو شب یہی ہو اپنا حال, (مرحبا) x۲

Mehfil sajao, Naate sunao
Aaqa ki aamad ki, Dhoome machao
Rozo shab yahi ho apna haal, (Marhaba) x2

Host/organize events and recite the praisings of Prophet Muhammad (pbuh), Rejoice in the arrival of the Master, We spend our day and night like this

CHORUS

عاشق کے دل جگمگانے لگے ہیں

دیکھو زرا، مسکرانے لگے ہیں

شاہکارِ ربِ ذولجلال, (مرحبا) x۲

Aashiq ke dil, Jag magane lage hai
Dekho zara, Muskurane lage hai
Shahkaare Rabbe Zuljalal, (Marhaba) x2

Hearts of lovers are shining with light, look they are all happy and smiling, O Masterpiece of the Lord of Majesty (Allah (AJ)), Greetings

CHORUS

صدقہ ولادت کا ،جلوا دِکھا دو

دل کی لگی، اب تو آقا بجھا دو

دِکھلا دو اپنا اب جمال, (مرحبا) x۲

Sadqa viladat ka, Jalwa dikha do
Dil ki lagi, Abb to aaqa bujha do
Dikhla do apna abb Jamal, (Marhaba) x2

For the sake of Your holy birth, show us Your magnificence and gaze upon us, O Master, put down the fire of Your love in my heart, feed the thirst of our hearts, O Master, Show us Your magnificent beauty, Greetings

CHORUS

جود و سخاوت ہے ،عادت تمہاری
پھیلائے دامن، کھڑے ہیں بکھاری
کر دو کرم، آمنہ کے لال, (مرحبا) x۲

Judo sakhawat hey, Aadat tumhari
Pehilaye daman, Khade hai bhikari
Kar do karam, Amina ke laal, (Marhaba) x2

Generosity is Your habit, beggars are standing in front of Your door,
Have mercy upon us O Son of Amina (Prophet's Mother), Greetings

CHORUS

Ya Muhammad Noore Mujassam

یا محمد نورِ مجسم

(O Muhammad, the Manifested Light)

يا حبيبى يا مولائ)x۲   (يا محمد نورِ مجسم

تنويرِ جمالِ خدائى   تصويرِ كمالِ محبت

يا محمد نورِ مجسم

(Ya Muhammad Noore Mujassam   **Ya Habibi Ya Mawlayee) x2**
Tasweere Kamale Muhabbat   **Tanveere Jamale Khudayee**
Ya Muhammad Noore Mujassam

O Muhammad (pbuh), You Embodied the light, O Beloved and Lordly,
Image of perfect Love, The illuminated Lordly Beauty

تيرى كون كرے گا بڑائى) x۲   (تيرا وصف بياں هو كس سے) x۲

جبريلِ امين كى رسائى   (اس گردِسفرميں گم ہيں) x۲

(Tera wasf bayaa ho kis se) x2   **(Teri kon karega barayee) x2**
(Iss garde safar may gum hai) x2   **Jibreele Ameen ki rasayee**

Who has the ability to describe Your attributes, Who can increase Your honour,
In the dust of Your heavenly journey, even the Trustworthy Gabriel's access is lost
[He couldn't go further with Prophet Muhammad (pbuh) on the Night of Ascension]

CHORUS

يہ گُلُ اور گلُ كا، جوبن) x۲   (يہ رنگِ بہارِ گُلشن) x۲

اُس دھوون كى رانائ   (تيرے نورِ قدم كا دھوون) x۲

(Ye range bahare gulshan) x2   **(Ye gul or gul ka, joban) x2**
(Tere Noore qadam ka dhowan) x2   **Us dhowan ki ra'nayee**

The color of the garden in the spring, the flower and its youthfulness, It is from the light of
the dripping water of Your holy feet; that dripping water is shimmering

CHORUS

(ما أَجْمَاك تیری صورت) ۲x
(ما اکمالاک تیری عظمت) ۲x

(ما احسنک تیری سیرت) ۲x
تیری ذات میں گم ہے خدائی

(Ma ajmalaka, teri surat) x2
(Ma akmalaka teri 'azmat) x2

(Ma ah'sanaka teri seerat) x2
Teri zaat may gum hai Khudayee

Your Face is the perfection of beauty; Your personality is the perfection of manners Your Magnificence is the absolute perfection; Lordship is lost in Your essence

CHORUS

(اے مظہرِ شانِ جمالی) ۲x
(مجھے حشر میں کام آجائے) ۲x

(اے خواجہ و بندہِ عالی) ۲x
میرا ذوقِ سخن آرائی

(Aay mazhare shaane jamali) x2
(Mujhe hashr may kaam aajaye) x2

(Aay Khwaja o Banda e 'Aali) x2
Mera zowqe sukhan aarayee

O Manifestation of perfect Beauty, O Master and the highest servant of Allah (AJ), I hope my eloquent way of praising upon You, will come in handy on the Last Day

CHORUS

(تو رئیس روزِ شفاعت) ۲x
(ہم سب کو تجھ سے نسبت) ۲x

(تو امیرِ لُطف و عنایت) ۲x
ہم غلام ہیں تو آقائ

(Tu rayise roze shafa'at) x2
(Hum sub ko, tujhse nisbat) x2

(Tu amire lutf o 'inayat) x2
Hum ghulam hai, tu aaqayee

You are the Leader of day of intercession; You are owner of gracious compassion and kindness, This reciter belongs to you, he is a slave and you are the Master

CHORUS

Pukaro Ya Rasul Allah

پکارو یا رسول اللہ

(Call Upon the Messenger of Allah)

(تیرا کھاواں میں تیرے گیت گاواں یا رسول اللہ) x۲

(Tera khavaa may teray geet, Gawaa Ya Rasul Allah) x2

I eat from your provision and sing your song, O Messenger of God

---

تیرا میلاد میں کیوں نہ مناواں یا رسول اللہ

یا رسول اللہ یا حبیب اللہ پکارو

یا رسول اللہ یا حبیب اللہ

Tera Milad may kiyo na manawaa, Ya Rasul Allah
Ya Rasul Allah, Ya Habib Allah, Pukaro
Ya Rasul Allah, Ya Habib Allah

Why shouldn't I celebrate your birthday, O Messenger of God
O Messenger of God, O Beloved of God, Say it!
O Messenger of God, O Beloved of God

(حلیمہ گھر کدی ویکھے، کدی سرکار نوں ویکھے) x۲

میں کیڑی سیج تیرے لیی سجاواں یا رسول اللہ

(Halima ghar kadi waikhay, kadi sarkar no waikhay) x2
May kairi saige teray lay, sajawaa Ya Rasul Allah

Halima (Prophet's wet nurse) sees the shining beauty of our Master in her house, She wonders, "What type of a palace should I decorate for you, O Messenger of God?"

CHORUS

(غلامِ احمدِ مختار، تو پہچانے جائیں گے) x۲

کہ محشر میں بھی ہو گا، اُن کا نعرہ یا رسول اللہ

(Ghulamay Ahmade Mukhtaar, tu peh' chaney jayengay) x2
Kay mehshar may bhi hoga, unka Nara "Ya Rasul Allah!"

The servants of Ahmad (pbuh), the Independent One, will be clearly known
As their slogan, even in the day of judgement will be, O Messenger of Allah (AJ)!

CHORUS

(سنا ہے آپ ہر عاشق ،کے گھر تشریف لاتے ہیں) x۲
کہ ہو میرے گھر میں بھی چراغاں یا رسول اللہ

(Suna hai Aap har aashiq, kay gharr tashreef laatey hai) x2
Kay ho meray ghar may bhi, charaghaa Ya Rasul Allah

I have heard that you come to the house (in the heart) of every lover of yours, I hope my
heart will also be illuminated with your presence, O Messenger of God

CHORUS

(نہ لے جب تک تمہارا نام بخشِش ہو نہیں سکتی) x۲
وہ بخشا جائے گا جس نے پکارا یا رسول اللہ

Na lay jab tak tumhara naam, Bakhshish ho nahi sakti x2
Woh bakhsha jayegah jisney, Pukara Ya Rasul Allah

Forgiveness will not be granted, Until they mention your Holy Name, The one who calls
upon you and says O Messenger of God, will be forgiven

CHORUS

Ya Mustafa, Noorul Huda

يا مصطفىٰ نورُالہدىٰ

(O Chosen One, the Light of Guidance)

يا مصطفىٰ نورُ الہدىٰ

شمسُ الضّحىٰ کوئی نہیں

ثانی تیرا کوئی نہیں

بَدرُالدُجا کوئی نہیں

Ya Mustafa, Noorul Huda
Shamsud duha koyee nahee

Saani tera koyee nahee
Badrud duja koyee nahee

O Chosen One, the Light of Guidance, Prophet Muhammad (pbuh), There is no one like you. No one is the brightest sun, No one is the full moon on a dark night, except you

ختمِ رُسل خیرُالورا

آئینہِ حسنِ ازل

کوئی نہیں تیرا بدل

تیرے سوا کوئی نہیں

Khatem e Rasul, khairul wara
Ayeena e husni azal

Koyee nahee tera badal
Terey siwa, koyee nahee

The first in creation, the last of the Messengers, No one can replace you. The mirror of original beauty is no one but you

CHORUS

ہے محترم سب مُرسلیں

شاہِ اُمم کوئی نہیں

لیکن دو عالم میں کہیں

خیرُ الورا کوئی نہیں

Hay Muhtaram, sab Mursaleen
Shahi Umam koyee nahee

Laykin du 'Aalam may kahi
Khairul wara, koyee nahee

All the messengers are honoured and noble, But in both worlds no one is the King of the Nations except you, No one is the best of creation except you

CHORUS

جائیں کہاں ہم بے نوا

ہم بے کسوں کا آسرا

آقا تیرے در کے سوا

یا مصطفىٰ کوئی نہیں

Jayeh kaha, ham bey Nawa
Ham bay kaso ka aasera

Aqa teri dar ke siwa
Ya Mustafa, koyee nahee

We are helpless. Where can we go, O Master, except to your door? For us who have no one to rely on, our saviour/refuge is nobody except you, O Chosen One

CHORUS

تم سا کہاں ہے دوسرا   اے مظہرِ نورِ خدا

تم سا ہوا کوئی نہیں   تم ہو امامُ انبیاء

Eh Mazhare Noore Khuda   **Tumsa kaha, hay dosra**
Tum ho Imamul Anbiya   **Tumsa howa, koyee nahee**

O manifestation of the Divine's light, how could there be anyone like you? You are the
Leader of the Prophets, Nobody can resemble and be like you

CHORUS

An Nabi Sallu Alayh

انبي صلوا عليه

(Praise Upon the Prophet)

صلاوات الله عليه
كل من صلى عليه

انبي صلو اعليه
وينال البركات

Salawatullahi alayh
Kullu man salla alayh

AnNabi sallu alayh,
Wa yanalul barakah,

The Prophet (pbuh) praise Him! Allah (AJ) bestowed blessings upon him, And everyone who praises him, Will be granted blessings

---

يا رسول الله ،يا رسول الله
يا حبيب الله ،يا حبيب الله

Ya RasulAllah, Ya RasulAllah
Ya HabibAllah, Ya HabibAllah
O Messenger of Allah (AJ), O Beloved of Allah (AJ)

علمواعلم اليقن) x٢
الفَرَضَ الصلاة عليه

(انبي يا حاضرين
ان رب العالمين

(AnNabi ya hadireen,
Ana Rabbil 'Aalameen,

'alamu 'ilmal y'aqeen) x2
Afradas salat 'alayh

The Prophet (pbuh), O attendees, you should know with certainty that, The Lord of both worlds, made praising upon him an obligation

CHORUS

تم پہ کروڑوں درود
تم پہ کروڑوں درود
تم پہ کروڑوں درود
تم پہ کروڑوں درود

کعبے کے بدرُالدجیٰ
طیبہ کے شمسد الُدحیٰ
شافعِ روزِ جزا
دافِعیٰ جملہ بلاء

Ka'abe Ke Badrud Duja
Tayba Ke Shamsud Duha
Shafiye Roze Jaza
Dafiye Jumla Bala,

Tum Pay Karoro Durood
Tum Pay Karoro Durood
Tum Pay Karoro Durood
Tum Pay Karoro Durood

O Full Moon of Ka'bah, O Bright Sun of Madina, O Intercessor of the day of judgment, O Demolisher of all affliction, billions of praisings be upon you

CHORUS

Hub e Rasul | Shaykh Nurjan Mirahmadi | www.nurmuhammad.com | staffsmc@gmail.com

تم سے جہاں کا نظام
تم پہ کروڑوں سلام
تم ہو جواد و کریم
بھیک ہو داتا عطا

تم پہ کروڑوں درود
تم پہ کروڑوں درود
تم ہو رؤوف و رحیم
تم پہ کروڑوں درود

Tum Se Jaha Ka Nizaam
Tum Pay Karoro Salam
Tum Ho Jawad o Kareem
Bheek ho Data Ataa

Tum Pay Karoro Durood
Tum Pay Karoro Durood
Tum Ho Rawofo Raheem
Tum Pay Karoro Durood

The system of the universes is kept by you, billions of praises be upon you, You are the generous giver, You are the kind and merciful, Give us your blessing as a charity O mighty giver, billions of praisings be upon you

CHORUS

Ya Shahe Umam

یا شاہِ اُمم

(O King of All Nations)

(یا شاہِ اُمم   (اِک نظرِ کرم)x۲

موری لاج تمہارے ہاتھ   سرکار

(Ya Shahe Umam,   **ek nazare karam) x2**
Mori laaj tumhare haath,   **Sarkaar**

O King of all nations, have a gaze of mercy upon us,
Gaze upon us with one blessed gaze, My honour is in your hand, O Master

---

موری نیا لگا دو اپنے کرم سے پار، سرکار

موری نیا لگا دو اپنے کرم سے پار

(صلی اللہ سیدالمُرسلین) x۴

Mori nayya laga do apne karam se paar, Sarkaar
Mori nayya laga do apne karam se paar
(SallAllah Sayyedul Mursaleen) x4

Push my sinking boat to the shore with your mercy, O Master, peace be upon you,
O Master of the Messengers (Prophet Muhammad (pbuh))

ٹوٹی ہوئی آس ہوں میں   دکھ سے بھرا دل ہے میرا

نظرِ کرم بحرِ خدا   کوئی نہیں تیرے سوا

(صلی اللہ سیدالمُرسلین) x۴

Tooti howi aas hu may,   **Dukh se bhara dil hay mera**
Nazre karam behre Khuda,   **Koyi nahi tere siwa**
(SallAllah Sayyedul Mursaleen) x4

I have lost all my hopes, my heart is filled with sorrow, Have a gaze of mercy on me, for
the sake of God, I have no one except you, Peace be upon you,
O Master of the Messengers

(غم خوارِ جہاں   (تسکینِ جاں)x۲

اِک شب تو مجھے بھی ہو   دیدار

(Ghamkhare jaha,   **Taskeene jaa) x2**
Ek shab tu mujhe bhi ho,   **Deedar**

You are the Supporter/Consoler of the world, You comfort the soul,
Bless me with your presence, one night

CHORUS

جس کی ہوا مُشکِ خُتن   باغِ ارم شہر تیرا

روحِ بیاں جان سخن   نام تیرا صلے علیٰ

(صلی اللہ سیدالمُرسلین) x۴

Baaghe Eram sheher tera,   **Jiss ki hawa mushke khutan**

Naam tera Salle 'Alaa,   **Roohe baya jaane sukhan**

(SallAllah Sayyidul Mursaleen) x4

Garden of Eram is your city; its air has a heavenly fragrance,
Your name is the soul of speech and life of words, blessing be upon you

سب رنجو الم) x۲   (ہو دور میرے

اِک بار   پھر آو مدینے میں

(Ho door merey,   **Sab ranjo alam) x2**

Pihr awoo Madiney may,   **Ek baar**

May all the afflictions and difficulties be removed from me,
Then I would come to Madina at least once

CHORUS

رکھ لو بھرم رب کے حبیب   عاصی ہوں میں بگڑے نصیب

تم ہی تو ہو سب کے طبیب   روحِ ادب جانِ ادیب

(صلی اللہ سیدالمُرسلین) x۴

Aasi hoo may bigre naseeb,   **Rakh lo bharam Rab ke Habib**

Roohe adab jaane adeeb,   **Tumhi tu ho sab ke tabeeb**

(SallAllah Sayyidul Mursaleen) x4

I am a sinner with a bad destiny, Keep my dignity, O Lord's Beloved,
You are the soul of literature, You are the life of the writer/poet,
You are everyone's healer, Blessings be upon you

(تمہیں کیا ہے کمی

تم دونوں جہاں کے ہو

مکی مدنی)x۲

سرکار

(Tumhe kiya hai kami,

Tum dono jahan ke ho,

Makki Madani) x2

Sarkaar

You have no deficiency, O Master of Makkah and Madina;
You are the Owner of both worlds

CHORUS

Meri Dharkan May Ya Nabi

میری دھڑکن میں یا نبی

(In My Heartbeat is the Prophet)

(میری دھڑکن میں یا نبی   میری سانسوں میں یا نبی)x۲

(بولو یا نبی، یا نبی ،یا نبی) x۲

یا نبی، یا نبی، یا نبی

(Meri dharkan may Ya Nabi,   Meri saaso may Ya Nabi) x2
(Bolo Ya Nabi, Ya Nabi, Ya Nabiii) x2
Ya Nabi, Ya Nabi, Ya Nabi

In my every heartbeat is Prophet Muhammad (pbuh),
In my every breath is Prophet (pbuh)
Say it, call upon Him, O Prophet (pbuh), O Prophet (pbuh)

تیرا نام آ گیا ہے)x۲   (کوئی گفتگو ہو لب پر
یہ مقام آ گیا ہے   (تیری مدحٰ کرتے کرتے) x۲

(Koyi guftugu ho lab par,   Tera naam agaya hay) x2
(Teri midha kartay kartay) x2   Yea maqam agaya hay

In every conversation, your name is on my tongue,
By continuously praising you, I achieved this spiritual station

CHORUS

میری چشمِ تر کے اندر)x۲   (درِ مصطفیٰ کا منظر
کبھی شام آ گیا ہے   (کبھی صُبح آگیا ہے) x۲

(Dare Mustafa ka manzar,   Meri chashme tar ke andar) x2
(Kabhi subhu agaya hay) x2   Kabhi shaam agaya hay

The scene of the door of the Chosen One, is in my teary eyes,
Sometimes it comes in morning and sometimes it comes in evening

CHORUS

| رُخ مصطفیٰ کو دیکھیں)x۲ | (یہ طلب تھی انبیا کی |
| اُنھیں کام آگیا ہے | (یہ نماز کا وسیلہ) x ۲ |

| **Rukhe Mustafa ko dekhay) x2** | **(Ye talab thi Anbiya ki,** |
| **Unhe kaam agaya hay** | **(Ye namaz ka waseela) x2** |

All prophets had a wish to see the holy face of Prophet Muhammad (pbuh), The Salah (Daily Prayer) came in handy, and became a means to feel his Holy Presence. [Referring to Isra in the Night of Ascension, when all prophets prayed with Prophet Muhammad (pbuh)]

CHORUS

Kamli Wale Muhammad (saw)

کملی والے محمد (ص)

I Sacrifice My Life for Beloved Muhammad (pbuh)

(کملی والے محمد توں صدقے میں جاں) x۲

جنہاں آ کے غریباں دی باں پھڑ لئی

(Kamli Wale Muhammad to sadke may jaa) x2
Jinaa aa ke ghariba dee baa parh layee

I sacrifice my life for Beloved Muhammad (pbuh),
Who came and held the hand of the poor

(میری بخشش وسیلہ محمد دا ناں) x۲

جنہاں آ کے غریباں دی باں پھڑ لئی

(Meri bakhshish wasila, Muhammad da naa) x2
Jinaa aa ke ghariba dee baa parh layee

The name of Muhammad is the means for my foregiveness,
The one who came and held the hand of the poor

CHORUS

(ادے واجو دنیا تے پیارا نہیں) x۲

أدے ورگا کوئی جگ تے سہارا نہیں

(جے نہ ہوندے محمد نہ ہوندا جہاں) x۲

جنہاں آ کے غریباں دی باں پھڑ لئی

(Ode wajo koyi duniya te pyara nahi) x2
Ode warga koyi jag te sahara nahi
(Je na hownde Muhammad na hownda jahaa) x2
Jinaa aa ke ghariba dee baa parh layee

No one is more beautiful than him in the entire world,
No one can give support like him in this world,
If he wasn't there, there would be no universe,
The one who came and held the hand of the poor

CHORUS

(لایا بدواں نوں سینے کمال ہویا) x۲
کوئی حبشی توں حضرت بلال ہویا
(آئے در تے سوالی نوں کیتی نہیں ناں) x۲
جنہاں آ کے غریباں دی باں پھڑ لئی

(Laya badua nu seenay kamal hoya) x2
Koi Habshi tu Hazrat Bilal hoya
(Ay dar te sawali nu kiti nahi na) x2
Jinaa aa ke ghariba dee baan parh layee

He brought bedouins to his nearness and perfected them,
A slave Habshi became Master Bilal (who called people to prayer)
He never said no to anyone who came seeking at his door
The one who came and held the hand of the poor

CHORUS

(نال اُنگلی اِشارے تے چن توڑیا) x۲
گیا سورج اگاں ول پچھاں موڑیا
(کلمہ سوہنڑے محمد دا پڑھیا بُتاں) x۲
جنہاں آ کے غریباں دی باں پھڑ لئی

(Nal ungli ishare te chand toreya) x2
Geya suraj aga wal picha moreya
(Kalma Soni Muhammad da parya buta) x2
Jinaa aa ke ghariba dee baa parh layee

With the movement of his finger, the Moon split
He brought the Sun back to its position to turn back the time.
Even the idols of the Ka'bah beared witness to his prophecy and fell down to the
ground in submission.

CHORUS

Madani Madine Wale

مدنی مدینے والے

(The Master of Medina)

مجھے در پہ پھر بلانا)
(مئے عشق بھی پلانا) x٢
Madani Madine Waley) x2
Madani Madine Waley

مدنی مدینے والے)x٢
مدنی مدینے والے

(Mujhe Dar pay pihr bolana
(Maye ishq bhi pilana) x2

Madani Madine Waley) x2
Madani Madine Waley

مجھے در پہ پھر بلانا   مدنی مدینے والے

Mujhe dar pay pihr bolana   Madani Madine Waley

Call me at Your door once again, O Master of Madina
Give me the nectar of love, O Master of Madina

(میری آنکھ میں سمانا   مدنی مدینے والے)x٢
(بنے دل تیرا ٹھکانہ) x٢   مدنی مدینے والے
(مدنی مدینے والے) x٢

(Meri aankh may samana   Madani Madine Waley) x2
(Banay dil Tera tikhana) x2   Madani Madine Waley
(Madani Madine Waley) x2

Sooth my eyes with Your presence, O Master of Madina, Make my heart to be your
house, O Master and Resident of Madina

(تیری جب کہ دید ہو گی   جبھی میری عید ہو گی)x٢
(میرے خواب میں تم آنا) x٢   مدنی مدینے والے
(مدنی مدینے والے) x٢

(Teri jab ke deed hogi   Jabhi meri Eid hogi) x2
(Mere khwaab me tum aana) x2   Madani Madine Waley
(Madani Madine Waley) x2

When I will be blessed to see you, that would be my Eid (grand celebration)
Please come in my dreams, O Master of Madina

CHORUS

Hub e Rasul | Shaykh Nurjan Mirahmadi | www.nurmuhammad.com | staffsmc@gmail.com

تیرے آستاں سے بڑھ کر)۲x   (تیرے در سے شاہٗ بہتر

مدنی مدینے والے   (ہے بھلا کوئی ٹھکانہ) x۲

(مدنی مدینے والے) x۲

(Tere dar se Shaha behtar   Tere aastaan say barhkar) x2

(Hay bhala koyee thikana) x2   Madani Madine Waley

(Madani Madine Waley) x2

O King, better than your door, Better than your house,
Could there be any higher station to be at? O Master of Madina

CHORUS

تو ہی دو جہاں کا یاور)x۲   (تو ہی انبیاء کا سرور

مدنی مدینے والے   (تو ہی راہبرِ زمانہ) x۲

(مدنی مدینے والے) x۲

(Tu hee Anbiya ka Sarwar   Tu hee do jahaa ka Yaawar) x2

(Tu hee Rehbare zamana) x2   Madani Madine Waley

(Madani Madine Waley) x2

You are the Leader of Prophets; You are the helper/supporter of both worlds,
You are the Leader of all time/eras, O Master of Madina

سبھی سے میرے سرور)x۲   (تو خدا کے بعد بہتر

مدنی مدینے والے   (تیرا ہاشمی گھرانہ) x۲

(مدنی مدینے والے) x۲

(Tu Khuda ke baad behtar   Sabhi say mere Sarwar) x2

(Tera Hashmi gharana) x2   Madani Madine Waley

(Madani Madine Waley) x2

You are the best after Allah (AJ), above everyone, O my Leader,
Your family is Hashmi, O Master of Madina

CHORUS

(تیری فرش پر حکومت)۲x   تیری عرش پر حکومت

(تو شہنشاہِ زمانہ) x۲   مدنی مدینے والے

(مدنی مدینے والے) x۲

(Teri farsh par hukumat   Teri Arsh par hukumat) x2

(Tu ShahenShahe zamana) x2   Madani Madine Waley

(Madani Madine Waley) x2

Your Kingdom is on earth, Your Kingdom is on heavens, You govern heavens and earth,
You are the Ultimate King of all eras, O Master of Madina

CHORUS

(تیرا خُلق سب سے اعلیٰ)۲x   تیرا حُسن سب سے پیارا

(فدا تجھ پہ سب زمانہ) x۲   مدنی مدینے والے

(مدنی مدینے والے) x۲

(Tere Khulq sab say 'Aala   Tera Husn Sab say pyara) x2

(Fida tujh pay sab zamana) x2   Madani Madine Waley

(Madani Madine Waley) x2

Your manner and character is the utmost high, Your beauty is above all beauty,
May the whole world be sacrificed for you, O Master of Madina

CHORUS

Balighal Ulaa bi Kamalihi

بلَغ لعُلا بِكما لهِ

(He Reached the Highest Station)

كاشفدُجابجمالِه)x۲   (بلَغ لعُلا بِكما له
صلو علیہ والهِ   حسُنت جمیعُ خصالِهِ

بلَغ لعُلا بِكما لِه

(Balaghal ulaa bi kamalihi   **Kashafad duja bi jamalihi) x2**
Hasunat jamiu Khisaalihi   **Sallu 'alayhi wa Aalihi**

Balaghal ulaa bi kamalihi

He (Prophet Muhammad (pbuh)) reached the highest place by his Perfection; He moved darkness by his Beauty, His character/manners were excellent, Send blessin~~ upon him and his Family, He reached the highest station by his perfection

نہ بس اِک جان دو جہاں فدا   کروں تیرے نام پہ جان فدا
کروں کیا کروڑوں جہاں نہیں   دو جہاں سے بھی نہیں جی بھرا

Karo tayray naam pay jaan fida   **Na bas ayk jaan, do jahan fida**
Do jahan say bhi, nahii ji bhara   **Karun kya, karoro jahan nahee**

I sacrifice my life in your name, not only one life but both worlds be sacrificed for you, even both worlds are not enough, I shall sacrifice billions of worlds for you, He reached the highest station by his perfection

CHORUS

میرے بگڑے کام سنور گئے   تیرے ذکر کی ہیں یہ برکتیں
وہیں رحمتوں کا نزول ہے   جہاں تیری یاد ہو دل نشیں

Tayray zikr ki, hay yea barkatay   **Mayray bigray kam sawar gaye**
Jahaa tayri yaad ho dil nashee   **Wahi rahmato ka nazool hay**

Reciting your name has so many blessings, that all problems have been sorted, Wherever your name is mentioned, O Beloved, Blessings descend upon there, He reached the highest station by his perfection

CHORUS

تیرے چاند پر بھی سلام ہو
ملا تجھ کو ماہِ تمام ہے

ہو درود تجھ پہ بھی آمنہ
تیری گود کتنی عظیم ہے

Ho darood tuj pay bhi Amina
Tayri goad kitni azeem hay

Tayray chaand par bhi Salam ho
Mila tujh ko maahe tamaam hay

Salutation upon you, O Amina (Prophet's mother), and peace be upon your moon Prophet Muhammad (pbuh), How magnificent is your lap that you received the Full Moon, He reached the highest station by his perfection

CHORUS

ملے دو جہاں کی آبرو
وہ کہیں کہ ہم کو قبول ہے

ہے یہ آرزو جو ہو سُرخرو
میں کہوں غلام ہوں آپ کا

Hey yea aarzo, jo ho surkhuru
May kahu ghulam ho Apka

Milay do jahaa ki aabru
Wo kahay, kay hamko qabul hay

This is my wish and desire and I will attain the honour of both worlds, When I would say that I am your servant, and he would say I accept it, He reached the highest station by his perfection

CHORUS

Lagiya Ne Mojaa

لگیاں نے موجاں

(Generous Blessings are Upon Us)

(لگیاں نے موجاں ہنڑ لائی رکھیں سوہنڑیا) x ٢
(چنگے آں کے مندے آں) x ٢
نبھائی رکھی سوہنڑیا
لگیاں نے موجاں

(Lagiya ne moja hon laayi rakhi soniya) x2
(Changay aa, Ke mande aa) x2
Nibhayi rakhi soniya
Lagiya ne moja
Generous blessings are upon us, Keep on dressing us O Beloved,
Whether we are good or bad, Keep us with You O Beloved,
Generous blessings are upon us

آقا دے غلاماں دا میں   ادنیٰ غلام آں
(لوکی کہندے خاص مینوں   میں عاماں توں وی عام آں) x ٢
پردہ جے پایا ہے اے تے   پائی رکھیں سوہنڑ
(چنگے آں کے مندے آں) x ٢
نبھائی رکھی سوہنڑیا

Aaqa de ghulama da may,   **Adna ghulamaa**
(Loki kehnde khas mayno,   **May aamaa tu wee aamaa) x2**
Parda je paaya hai te,   **Paayi rakhi soniya**
(Changay aa, Ke mande aa) x2
Nibhayi rakhi soniya

I am the smallest servant of your real servants, O Master, people think I am special but I
am just a regular person, As you have been veiling my sins, keep on veiling, O Beloved,
Whether we are good or bad, Keep us with you, O Beloved

CHORUS

عملاں نے تولناں   حشر دیہاڑے جدوں

(کُج وی نہں بولنا)x۲   (شرم دے مارے میں تے

چھپائی رکھیں سوہنڑیا   کملی وچ اپنے

(چنگے آں کے مندے آں) x۲

نبھائی رکھی سوہنڑیا

Hashr dihare jaddo,   Amlaa ne tolna
(Sharm de maare may te,   Kujh wee ni bolna) x2
Kamli vich apney,   Chupayi rakhi soniya
(Changay aa, Ke mande aa) x2
Nibhayi rakhi soniya

When my deeds are judged on the Day of Judgment, I would be ashamed and can't say a single word, Hide me in your cloak on that day, O Beloved, Whether we are good or bad, Keep us with you, O Beloved

CHORUS

دکھڑا سنایا نہیں   کسے نوں میں اپنا

(سینے نال لایا نہیں)x۲   (تیرے باجو کسی مینوں

لائی رکھی سوہنڑیا   سینے نال لایا ای تے

(چنگے آں کے مندے آں) x۲

نبھائی رکھی سوہنڑیا

Kisay nu may apna,   Dukhra sunaya nayi
(Tere baajo kisse meno,   Seene naal laaya nayi) x2
Seene naal laaya aey te,   Laaye rakhi soniya
(Changay aa, Ke mande aa) x2
Nibhayi Rakhi Soniya

I have never told my grieving story to anyone, No one has ever held me and brought me to their proximity like you did, Now that you have brought me to your nearness O Beloved, always keep me near to your light, Whether we are good or bad, Keep us with you, O Beloved

CHORUS

نام تیرا لے کے آقا   شان اساں پائی اے

(تیرے ہتھ ڈور سائیاں   آپے ہی چڑھائی اے)x۲

چڑھی ہوئی گڈی نوں   چڑھائی رکھیں سوہنڑیا

(چنگے آں کے مندے آں) x۲

نبھائی رکھی سوہنڑیا

Naam tera le ke aaqa   **Shaan assaa payi yea**
(Teray haath dor saiyaa,   **Apay he charhai yea) x2**
Charhi hui guddi nu,   **Charhai rakhi soniya**
(Changay aa, Ke mande aa) x2
Nibhayi rakhi soniya

By mentioning and praising your Name O Master, I attained this high station, My thread is in your hand and you are the one raising it higher, As you have kept my kite (soul) flying, Keep it flying higher, O Beloved. Whether we are good or bad, Keep us with you, O Beloved

CHORUS

Allah Allah Allah Hu

الله الله الله ہو

> **(الله الله الله ہو لاَاِلٰہَ اِلاَّ ھُو) x۲**
>
> **(Allah Allah AllaHu, La illaha illaHu) x2**

(آمنہ بی بی کے گلشن میں
(پڑھتے ہیں صلی الله وسلم) x۲

(آئی ہے تازہ بہار)x۲
آج درودیوار نبی جی

(Amina bibi keh gulshan may,
(Parthay hai SallAllahu wa sallam) x2

(Aayee hai taza bahaar) x2
Aaj daro deewar, Nabi Jee

In the garden of Lady Amina (Mother of Prophet), A new spring has arrived,
All doors and walls are reciting salutations

CHORUS

وہ آیا دُرِ یتیم)x۲
صاحبِ خلقِ عظیم نبی جی

(بارہ ربیع الاول کو
(ماہِ نبوت مہرِ رسالت) x۲

(Baarah Rabbi ul Awwal ko,
(Maahe Nabuwwat, mehre risalat) x2

Woh aayah dure yateem) x2
Saahibe khulqe 'Azeem, Nabi Jee

He came to the world on 12th of Rabbi ul Awwal, He who is Healer of the Orphans, the
Spirit of Prophethood, the Protector of Prophecy, the Owner of the Best Manners

CHORUS

دو جگ کے سردار)۲
رحمت کے سرکار نبی جی

(حامدومحمود اور محمد
(جاں سے پیارا راج دُلارا) x۲

(Hamido Mahmood or Muhammad,
(Jaan sey pyaara, Raj dulaara) x2

Dow jag kay sardaar) x2
Rahmat kay sarkaar, Nabi Jee

Praiser, the Most Praised One, and Muhammad [Prophet Muhammad's (pbuh) holy
names], King of both worlds, More precious than my life, the beloved King,
Master of Mercy in creation

CHORUS

(يسين،طهٰ کملی والا
(حاضرو ناظر شاہدوقاسم) x ۲

(قراں کی تفسیر)x۲
آیا سراجُنُ منیر نبی جی

**(Yaseen, TaHa, kamli waala,
(Haziro Nazir, Shahido Qasim) x2**

**Qur'an ki tafseer) x2
Aaya sirajun munir, Nabi Jee**

Yasin, Taha [Prophet Muhammad's (pbuh) names], The Owner of the Veil,
The Qur'an and its description, The Present and the Witness, The Observer and the
Distributor, The Source of Guidance [Prophet Muhammad's (pbuh) names], He (pbuh)
has arrived

CHORUS

Rab Farmaya
رب فرمایا
(The Lord Said)

رب فرمایا محبوبا
اُوہ عرشی وی ،اُوہ فرشی وی

زمانے سارے تیرے نے
دیوانے سارے تیرے نے

Rab farmaya mehbooba
O Arshee wee, o farshee wee

Zamanai sarey terey nai
Deewane sarey terey nai

The Lord said to His Beloved, all worlds belong to you,
People of earth and heavens are all crazy about you

میں خالق ساری دنیا دا
کِسے منگتے نوں نہ موڑیں

تو مالک ساری دنیا دا
خزانے سارے تیرے نے

May Khaliq, saree duniya da
Kisay mangtay noo na moree

Tu Malik, saree duniya da
Khazanai sarey terey nai

I am the Creator of this universe, and you are the Owner of this universe, Don't return
any seeker, all treasures belong to you

اذاں ہووے نماز ہووے
جو گوجن ہر طرف سجناں

درود ہووے سلام ہووے
ترانے سارے تیرے نے

Azan howay, namaz howay
Jo goojan har taraf sajna

Durood howay, salaam howay
Taranay sarey terey nai

Whether its call to prayer, praising, salat (prayer) or salam (greetings/peace), Whatever
the echo is everywhere, it is all your anthems/songs

تیرے قبضے وچ دے چھڈیاں
ستارے چند تے سیارے

اوہ تقدیراں اوہ تدبیراں
نشانے سارے تیرے نے

Terey kabzay vich dey chadiya
Sitaray chand tey saiyaray

O taqdeera, o tadbeera
Nishaanay sarey terey nai

All destinies and decisions are in your possessions,
Stars, Moon and Galaxies are all your signs

میں شاہ رگ توں وی اقرب ہاں   توں جاناں تو وی ہے نیڑے

جو دل میں سینیاں اندر   ٹھکانے سارے تیرے نے

May shahrag tu wee akrab haa   **Tu jaanan ton wee hay nayray**

Jo dil may seenia andar   **Tihkanai sarey terey nai**

I am closer to the jugular vein, and you are closer to the soul
All the hearts are a house for you

امیراں نال کر لیندا   محبت ہر کوئی ناصر

غریباں نال محبوبا   یارانے سارے تیرے نے

Ameera naal kar lenda   **Mohabbat har koi nasir**

Ghareeba naal mehbooba   **Yaaranai sarey terey nai**

Everyone can love the rich and wealthy,
Every friendship to the poor is your friendship

Sayyedina wa Mawlana Muhammadin

سيدنا ومولانا محمدٍ

(Our Master Prophet Muhammad (pbuh))

(الهمَ صل على سيدنا ومولانا محمدٍن) x۳

(Allahumma Salay 'ala, Sayyedina wa Mawlana Muhammadin) x3

O Allah (AJ) send blessings upon our Lord and Master Muhammad (pbuh)

أُتھے رہندا سدا سویرا اے)x۲   (جتھے میرے حضور دا ڈیرہ اے
انہوں چھڈ دیو اے میرا اے   (وچ قبر دے آقا آکھن گے) x۲

(Jithay mayre Huzoor da daira aiy,   **Uthay rehnda sada sawaira aiy) x2**
(Vich qabar de Aaqa aakhan gai) x2   **Aaeno chad daiyo aiy te Mayra aiy**

Where my beloved is resting (Madina), the lights always live there,
Master will say this, in my grave allow him as he is one of mine

CHORUS

متھے چمکنے لاٹ نورانی اے)x۲   (مکُھ چند بدن شعشانی اے
مخمور اکھیں ہن مد بھریاں   (کالی زلف تے اکھ مستانی اے) x۲

(Mukh chand badan shashaani aiy,   **Mathay chamke laat noorani aiy) x2**
(Kali zulf teh, akh mastani aiy) x2   **Makhmoor akhiyan madhbhariyan**

His holy face is the Moon and his holy body is like a shining jewel,
A beam of light is shining from his holy forehead, His hairs are dark black
and his eyes are dazzling and full of ecstasy

CHORUS

انہوں کون مٹاون والا اے)x۲   (لج پال جدا رکھوالا اے
جھڑا توڑنبھاوڑن والا اے   (ساڈی اُس سوہنڑے نال لگ گئی اے) x۲

(Lajpaal jidda rakhwala aiy,   **Oanhoon koon mitawan wala aiy) x2**
(Sadi os sohne naal lag gai aiy) x2   **Jirra Tor Nibhawan walaa aiy**

The Mighty Saviour is his protector, who can dare challenge him, We have bonded with
the One, Who has completed his covenant/commitments

CHORUS

Hub e Rasul | Shaykh Nurjan Mirahmadi | www.nurmuhammad.com | staffsmc@gmail.com

سب سے بالا و اعلیٰ ہمارا نبی)x۲   (سب سے اولیٰ و اعلیٰ ہمارا نبی

دونوں عالم کا دولہا ہمارا نبی   (اپنے مولا کا پیارا ہمارا نبی) x۲

Sab se baala ho aala hamara Nabi) x2   (Sab se awla ho aala hamara Nabi,

Dono aalam ka dhola hamara Nabi   (Apne mawla ka piyara hamara Nabi) x2

Our Prophet is the First and Most High, His station is above all prophets, Our Prophet is the Beloved of his Lord, He is the Prince of both worlds

CHORUS

Tu Kuja Man Kuja
تو کجا من کجا
(You are Everything and I am Nothing)

(تو کجا من کجا) x۴

(Tu kuja, man kuja) x4

You are divinely manifestation, You are dressed with beautific heavenly reality,
O Prophet Muhammad (pbuh), You are everything and I am absolutely nothing

(تو امیرِ حرم میں فقیرِ عجم) x۲
(تیرے گُن اور یہ لب،میں طلب ہی طلب) x۲
تو عطا ہی عطا

(Tu Amire Haram, may faqeer e ajam) x2
(Tere gun aur yeh lab, may talab he talab) x2
Tu ata hee, ataa

You are the King of heavenly sanctuary and I am a poor foreigner. My lips are unworthy
of singing your lofty praises. I am always in need and asking you for favours and support.
You are filled with blessings and generosity and you always keep giving.

CHORUS

(الہام ہے جامہ تیرا) x۲
(منبر ترا عرشِ بریں) x۲

(قرآں عمامہ ہے تیرا) x۲
یا رحمت العلامیں

(Ilhaam hay, jaamah tera) x2
(Minbar tera Arsh e bareen) x2

(Quran imaama, hay tera) x2
Ya rehmatal lil alameen

You are gloriously dressed with the Divine revelation. The holy Quran is your crown and
the exalted turban. The Divinely Throne is your pulpit, O mercy to all creation.

CHORUS

(تو حقیقت ہے میں صرف احساس ہوں) x۲

(تو سمندر میں بھٹکی ہوئی پیاس ہوں) x۲

(میرا گھر خاک پر اور تیری رہ گزر) x۲

صدرۃالمنتہیٰ

(Tu haqeeqat hay, may sirf ehsaas hoo) x2

(Tu samandar, may bhakti huwi pyaas hoo) x2

(Mera ghar khaak par, or teri rahguzar) x2

Sidratul Muntahaa

You are the reality and the truth, and I am merely an illusion. You are the divinely ocean of mercy and ever-living, and I am a wandering seeker, thirsty for your mercy. My house is on the material world of dirt and clay, and your residence beyond heavens "at the Lote Tree of the farthest limit and utmost boundary" of divinely presence. (Holy Quran 53:14).

CHORUS

(آوازِ حق خطبہ تیرا) x۲   (خیر البشر رُتبہ تیرا) x۲

(سائیس جبریلِ امین) x۲   (آفاق تیرے سامعیں) x۲

یا رحمت العالمیں

(Khair ul Bashar rutbah tera) x2   **(Awaaz e Haqq khutbah tera) x2**

(Aafaaq tere saamaeen) x2   **(Saais Jibreel e Ameen) x2**

Ya rahmat ul il alameen

Your rank is the Best of Mankind, Your holy speech is the Truth of divinely presence. All the inhabitants of the heavens are your audience. The trustworthy Archangel Gabriel (as) was created to be of service to you and take care of all your needs, O mercy to all creation

CHORUS

(خوشبو تیری عرفان ہے) x۲   (نسبت تیری ایمان ہے) x۲

قران ہی قران ہے   (تصویر تیرے خلق کی) x۲

یا رحمت العالمیں   تو حاصلِ دنیا و دیں

(Nisbat teri, Imaane hay) x2   **(Khushbu teri, irfaane hay) x2**

(Tasveer terey, khulq ki) x2   **Quran hee, Quran hay**

Tu hasil e Dunya o Deen   **Ya rahmatal lil alameen**

Station of Iman (faith) is to love you more than myself, my parents and everyone else. Your beautiful fragrance is the essence of Gnosticism. As your Lord described "you are of a magnificent character". (Quran 68:4) You are the embodiment and reality of Walking Holy Quran. My whole life and my aim in both worlds is to attain your love and satisfaction, O mercy to all creation

CHORUS

(آنکھیں تیری بابِ حرم) x۲

یا رحمت العالمیں

(خوشبو تیری جوۓ کرم) x۲

(نورِ ازل تیری جبیں) x۲

(Khushbu teri, jooye karam) x2
(Noor e azal, teri jabeen) x2

(Ankay teri, baab e Haram) x2
Ya rahmatal lil alameen

Your beautiful fragrance is the river of blessing. Your holy eyes are the door to Mulk wal Malakut (heavens and earth). The pre-eternal divinely light is your holy forehead, O mercy to all creation

CHORUS

(تو ہے احرامِ انوار باندھے ہوۓ) x۲

(میں درودوں کی دستار باندھے ہوۓ) x۲

(کعبۓ عشق تو، میں تیرے چار سو) x۲

تو اثر میں دعا

(Tu hay ahraam e anwaar baandhe huee) x2
(May duroodon ki dastaar baandhe huee) x2
(Kaaba e ishq tu, may tere chaar su) x2
Tu asar may dua

You are wrapped in divinely light. You are the embodiment of the 'Secret of the Lights and the Light of the Secrets'. I wear on my head a crown of salutation and praising upon you, which gives me light and honour. You are the Ka'ba of love and I circumambulate around you. Even my praising and prayers are only cleansed through your intercession.

CHORUS

Mother of Supplications

أُمُّ الدُّعَاء

سَيِّدِي لِمَوْلَانَا اَلشَّيْخْ عَبْدُاللهِ الْفَائِزِ الْدَاغِسْتَانِي

Mawlana Shaykh Abdullah al Fa'iz ad Daghestani's Supplication
By: Mawlana Shaykh Hisham Kabbani

اَللَّهُمَّ أَجْعَلْ أَوَّلَ مَجْلِسِنَا هَذَا صَلَاحًا وَ أَوْسَطَهُ فَلَاحًا وَ آخِرَهُ نَجَاحًا. اَللَّهُمَّ أَجْعَلْ أَوَّلَهُ رَحْمَةً وَ أَوْسَطَهُ نِعْمَةً وَ آخِرَهُ تَكْرِيمَةً وَمَغْفِرَةً. اَلْحَمْدُ لله الَّذِي تَوَاضَعَ كُلّ شَيْءٍ لِعَظَمَتِه وَ ذَلَّ كُلّ شَيْءٍ لِعِزَّتِه وَخَضَعَ كُلّ شَيْءٍ لِمُلْكِه وَأَسْتَسْلَمَ كُلّ شَيْءٍ لِقُدْرَتِه. وَ اَلْحَمْدُ لله الَّذِي سَكَنَ كُلّ شَيْءٍ لِهَيْبَتِه وَأَظْهَرَ كُلّ شَيْءٍ بِحِكْمَتِه وَتَصَاغَرَ كُلّ شَيْءٍ لِكِبْرِيَائِه . اَللَّهُمَّ أَيْقِظْنَا فِي أَحَبّ السَاعَةِ إِلَيْكَ يَا وَدُودُ يَا "ذُو الْعَرْشِ الْمَجِيدِ فَعَّالٌ لِمَا يُرِيدُ . هَلْ أَتَاكَ حَدِيثُ الْجُنُودِ . فِرْعَوْنَ وَثَمُودَ. بَلِ الَّذِينَ كَفَرُوا فِي تَكْذِيبٍ. وَاللَّهُ مِنْ وَرَائِهِمْ مُحِيطٌ. بَلْ هُوَ قُرْآنٌ مَجِيدٌ . فِي لَوْحٍ مَحْفُوظٍ " (سُورَةُ الْبُرُوجِ ٨٥ : ١٥ـ٢٢)

Allahuma aj'al awwala majlesina hadha salahan wa awsatahu falahan wa akhirahu najahan. Allahuma aj'al awwala hu rahmatan wa awsatahu ni'matan wa akhirahu takrimatan wa maghfirah. Alhamdulila hiL 'ladhi tawad'a kulli shayin li 'azamatihi wa dhalla kulli shayin li 'izzatihi wa khad'a kulli shayin li mulkihi w'astaslama kulli shayin li qudratih. Alhamdulila hiL 'ladhi sakana kulli shayin li haybatihi wa azhara kulli shayin bi hikmatihi wa tasaghara kulli shayin li kibriyaihi. Allahuma 'ay qizna fi ahabbi sa'ati ilayka ya Wadud, ya "dhu'l 'arsh il Majid. fa'alul lima yurid. Hal ataka hadithul junud. Fir'awna wa Thamuda baliL ladhina kafaru fi takdhibin. Wa Allahu min waraihim muhit. Bal huwa Quranun Majid. Fi lawhin mahfuz."

O our Lord! Make the beginning of this gathering goodness, its middle happiness, and its end success. O our Lord! Make its beginning mercy, its middle bounty, and its ending generosity and forgiveness. All praise be to Allah (AJ) who humbled everything before His Greatness, made all things subservient before His Honour, brought low all things before His Kingship, and made all things submit to His Power. And all praise to Allah (AJ) who made all things tranquil before His Majesty, and made everything appear through His wisdom, and humbled all things before His Pride. O our Lord! Wake us in the time most beloved to Yourself, O Loving One, O *Lord of the Throne of Glory, Doer (without let) of all that He intends. as the story reached thee, of the forces Of Pharaoh and the Thamud? And yet the Unbelievers (persist) in rejecting (the Truth)! But Allah (AJ) doth encompass them from behind! Nay, this is a Glorious Qur'an, (Inscribed) in Preserved Tablet!"* (Holy Quran, Al Buruj, The Mansions of Stars; 85:15-22)

اَللَّهُمَّ اغْفِرْلِيْ ذُنُوْبِيْ وَ لِوَالِدَيَّ كَمَا رَبَّيَانِيْ صَغِيْرًا وَلِجَمِيْعِ الْمُؤْمِنِيْنَ وَالْمُؤْمِنَاتِ، وَالْمُسْلِمِيْنَ وَالْمُسْلِمَاتِ، الْأَحْيَاءِ مِنْهُمْ وَ الْأَمْوَاتِ، وَ"اغْفِرْ لَنَا وَلِإِخْوَانِنَا اَلَّذِيْنَ سَبَقُوْنَا بِالْإِيْمَانِ وَلَا تَجْعَلْ فِيْ قُلُوْبِنَا غِلًّا لِلَّذِيْنَ اَمَنُوْا، رَبَّنَا إِنَّكَ رَؤُوْفٌ رَحِيْمٌ يَا أَرْحَمَ الرَّاحِمِيْنَ." (سُوْرَةُ اَلْحَشْرِ ٥٩:١٠)

Allahuma 'ghfirli dhunubi wa li walidayya kama rabbiyani saghiran wa li jami'il muminina wal muminati, wal muslimina wal muslimati, al ah ya'ye min hum wal amwat, wa"ghfir lana wa li ikhwaninaL ladhina sabaquna bil imani, wa la taj'al fi qulubana ghillan liL ladhina amanu rabbana innaka Ra'ufun Rahim ya arham ar rahimin."

O Allah (AJ) forgive me my sins and my parents' just as they raised me when I was small and to all the believers, men and women, and all the Muslims, men and women, both the living among them and the dead, *Our Lord! Forgive us, and our brethren who came before us into the Faith, and leave not, in our hearts, rancour against those who have believed. Our Lord! Thou art indeed Full of Kindness, Most Merciful."* (Holy Quran al-Hashr (The Exile), 59:10) O Most Merciful of those who show mercy!

اَللَّهُمَّ بِجَاهِ حَبِيْبِكَ الْمُصْطَفَى وَرَسُوْلِكَ الْمُرْتَضَى، وَبِجَاهِ أَوْلِيَائِكَ الْكِرَامِ، وَبِجَاهِ صَحَابَتِهِ الْفِخَامِ، وَبِجَاهِ سُلْطَانِ الْأَوْلِيَا سَيِّدِيْ مَوْلَانَا اَلشَّيْخْ عَبْدُاللهِ اَلْفَائِزْ اَلدَّاغِسْتَانِي وَسَيِّدِيْ مَوْلَانَا اَلشَّيْخْ مُحَمَّد نَاظِمْ عَادِلَ الْحَقَّانِي، وَمَوْلَانَا اَلشَّيْخْ هِيشَامْ اَلْقَبَّانِي، أَنْ لَا تَدَعَ فِيْ مَجْلِسِنَا هَذَا ذَنْبًا إِلَّا غَفَرْتَهُ، وَلَا دَيْنًا إِلَّا قَضَيْتَهُ، وَلَا مَرِيْضًا إِلَّا شَفَيْتَهُ، وَ لَا حَاجَةً مِنْ حَوَائِجِ اَلدُّنْيَا وَالْأَخِرَةِ إِلَّا قَضَيْتَهَا وَيَسَّرْتَهَا. اَللَّهُمَّ يَسِّرْ أُمُوْرَنَا وَاَقْضِ دُيُوْنِنَا، وَفَرِّجْ هُمُوْمَنَا وَفَرِّجْ كُرُوْبَنَا، وَ ثَبِّتْ أَقْدَامَنَا وَاَنْصُرْنَا عَلَى أَنْفُسِنَا وَعَلَى الْقَوْمِ الْكَافِرِيْنَ.

Allahuma bi jahi habibikal Mustafa wa rasulikal Murtada, sallalahu 'alayhi wa sallam wa bi jahi awliya' yekal kiram wa bi jahi sahabatihil fikham wa bi jahi sultan al awliya sayyidi Mawlana ash Shaykh 'Abdullah al Fa'izi ad Daghestani wa sayyidi Mawlana ash Shaykh Muhammad Nazim Adil al Haqqani, wa Mawlana ash Shaykh Hisham Qabbani, an la tad'a fi majlisina hadha dhanban illa ghafartahu, wa la deenan illa qadaytahu, wa la maridan illa shafaytahu, wa la hajatan min hawayej ad dunya wal akhirat illa qadaytaha wa yassartaha. Allahuma yassir umurana wa aqdi duyunina wa farrij humumana wa farrij kurubana, wa thabbit aqdamana wan surna 'ala anfusina wa 'alal qawmil kafirin.

O Allah (AJ) for the sake of Your Beloved Chosen Prophet and Your Prophet with whom You are pleased, and for the sake of Your honoured saints and for the sake of the Prophet's inestimable companions and for the sake the Sultan of Saints our master Shaykh 'Abdullah al Fa'iz ad Daghestani and my master Shaykh Muhammad Nazim al Haqqani do not leave anyone in this gathering whose sins have not been forgiven, and no debt that has not been forgiven, and no ill one who has not been cured and no need of this life or the Hereafter except that You have judged it and made it easy. O Allah (AJ) make our affairs easy and pay off our debts and relieve our distress and allay our concerns and make steadfast our feet and give victory over ourselves and on the unbelieving enemies within.

اَللَّهُمَّ اشْفِنَا وَاشْفِ مَرْضَانَا وَ مَرْضَى الْمُسْلِمِينَ، وَعَافِنَا وَ عَافِ مَرْضَانَا وَ مَرْضَى الْمُسْلِمِينَ، وَتَقَبَّلْ مِنَّا يَا رَبَّنَا يَا الله وَأَمِدَنَا بِعُمْرِنَا لِإِدْرَاكَ صَاحِبِ الزَّمَانْ سَيِّدِنَا مَهْدِيْ عَلَيْهِ السَّلَامْ، وَ سَيِّدِنَا عِيْسَى عَلَيْهِ السَّلَامْ، وَارْزُقْنَا شَفَاعَةَ النَّبِيْ الْمُصْطَفَى عَلَيْهِ أَفْضَلَ الصَّلَاةِ وَالسَّلَامْ، وَاجْعَلْنَا أَنْ نَرَاهُ فِيْ الدُّنْيَا وَ فِي الْأَخِرَةِ وَاسْقِنَا مِنْ حَوْضِهِ شَرْبَةً هَنِيْئَةً مَرِيْئَةً لَا نَظْمَوْ بَعْدَهَا أَبَدَا.

Allahum ma'shfina washfi mardana wa mardal muslimin, wa 'afina wa 'afi mardana wa mardal muslimin, wa taqabbal minna ya rabbana ya Allah, wa amidana bi 'umrina li idrak Sahib az Zaman Sayyidina Muhammad al Mahdi 'alayhis salam, wa Sayyidinna 'Isa 'alayhis salam, warzuqna shafa'a tAnNabi al Mustafa 'alayhi afdalas salati was salam, waj'al lana an narahu fiddunya wa fi'l akhirati w'asqina min hawdihi sharbatan haniyattan mariyattan la nazmao b'ada ha abada.

O Allah (AJ) (Allahuma) heal our sickness (physical and spiritual), and heal our loved ones, and everyone who is sick. And O Allah (AJ), give good health to us, to our loved ones, and to everyone who is sick. And please accept from us (our prayers/plea) oh our Lord, O Allah (AJ).

And extend our life to reach the time of honorable, the owner of era/end of time, our Master Mahdi (as), and our Master Isa (Jesus) (as). And grant us the intercession of the Chosen One, Prophet Muhammad (pbuh). And grant us the blessings of being in the holy presence of Prophet Muhammad (pbuh) in here and in hereafter. And please quench our thirst from the sweet nectar of Your heavenly fountain [Kawthar – Fountain of Abundance], so that we would never feel thirst ever after.

اَللَّهُمَّ إِنَّا نَسْأَلُكَ مِنْ خَيْرِ مَا سَأَلَكَ مِنْهُ سَيِّدِنَا مُحَمَّدٍ (ص) وَ نَسْتَعِيْذُكَ مِنْ شَرِّ مَا اسْتَعَاذَكَ مِنْهُ سَيِّدِنَا مُحَمَّدْ(ص) وَاَلْحَمْدُ لِلّٰهِ رَبِ الْعَالَمِيْنْ. رَبَّنَا تَقَبَّلْ مِنَّا بِحُرْمَةِ مَنْ أَنْزَلْتَ عَلَيْهِ سِرِّ سُوْرَةُ الْفَاتِحَةْ.

Allahuma inna nas'aluka min khayri ma sa'alaka minhu sayyidina Muhammadin (sallAllahu 'alayhi wa sallam) wa nast'ayidhuka min sharri masta'adhaka minhu sayyidina Muhammad (sallAllahu 'alayhi wa sallam). w'al hamdulillahi rabbil 'alamin. Rabbana taqabbal minna bi hurmati man anzalta 'alayhi sirri suratu'l Fatihah. (Recite first Chapter of Quran, Al Fatiha (The Opener))

O Allahuma (Allah (AJ)), we ask You for all the best things that our master Prophet Muhammad (pbuh) asked for. And we seek refuge and protection from all the evilness that our master Prophet Muhammad (saws) sought refuge from. And all praises be to the Lord of the Worlds. Oh our Lord, please accept from us (these supplications) by the blessings of the one (Prophet Muhammad (pbuh)), upon whom You sent the secrets of the Surat Al Fatiha (The Opener) [Recite the first chapter of holy Quran]

CPSIA information can be obtained
at www.ICGtesting.com
Printed in the USA
LVHW020739160322
713569LV00008B/989